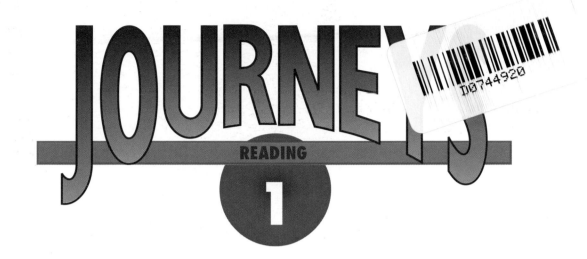

JOURNEYS
READING 1

RONI LEBAUER

STEVEN BROWN SERIES EDITOR

Prentice Hall Asia ELT

Publishing Director: Stephen Troth
Acquisitions Editor: Nancy Baxer
Senior Editor: Nicola Miller
Editorial Production: Betty Bravo, Marketing Horizons
Production Manager: Oliver Lam

First published 1997 by
Prentice Hall Asia ELT
317 Alexandra Road
#04-01 IKEA Building
Singapore 159965

Printed in Singapore

Library of Congress Cataloging-in-Publication Data

Information is available from the publisher on request.

ISBN 0-13-171448-1 (Journeys Reading 1)

5 4 3 2 1
99 98 97

Contents

Text Credits

Unit 3   "A Full House" from "Full House" by Meg Grant in *People Weekly*, Fall 1991, volume 36

Unit 4   "Anita Roddick: Businesswoman" from "It's All Our Business" in *New Statesman and Society*, December 17/31, 1993

Unit 6   "Is Your Diet Healthy?" from "Leafy, Crunchy Spread Salutes the Salad" by Michelle Nicolosi in *The Orange County Register*, April 6, 1994

Unit 8   "The Power of Color" from "The Power of Color" by Leslie Kane in *Health*, July 1982

Unit 9   "The Clock is Ticking" from "How to Find the Time You Need" by Debra Wise in *Mademoiselle*, April 1994, volume 100; also from "Time for a Change" by Richard Laliberte in *Men's Health*, April 1994

Unit 11   "The Man Behind Blue Jeans" from "The National Business of Fame" by Peter Nulty in *Fortune*, April 4, 1994

Unit 12   "My Aching Head" from *The Complete Home Healer* by Angela Smyth, Harper San Francisco

Unit 13   "When Lost Twins Find Each Other" from "'Lost' Twins", in *Good Housekeeping*, October 1988

Unit 14   "QWERTY? Why?" from *Century of the Typewriter* by Wilfred A. Beeching, NY: St Martin's Press, 1974

Unit 16   "The Weather Forecaster or the Cat?" from "Feline Forecasters" by Elinor DeWire in *Weatherwise*, June/July 1992

Unit 17   "Same Time, Same Place" from "Millions of Monarchs" by Brad Darrach in *Life*, August 1993

Unit 18   "Are We Having Fun Yet?" from "A Stairway to Heaven, Hell for Runners" by Barry Bearak in *LA Times*, February 18, 1994

Unit 19   "Travel to the End of the Earth" from "Journey to the End of the Earth" by Rebecca Ketcham in *Women's Sports and Fitness*, March 1992; also "Polar Dare" by Priscilla Turner in *Ms.*, June 1989

Photo Credits

The Embassy of the Arab Republic of Egypt (p. 4 Omar; p. 60 Jamal; p. 112 Aziz)

The Body Shop/iMAGE Public Relations (p. 30 Anita Roddick, The Body Shop)

Mee Hee Hwang/Amanda Fox (p. 60 Kyung)

Cristy Grace (p. 90 Barbara and Ann)

From the Series Editor

Journeys is a twelve-book, three-level, skills-based series for EFL/ESL learners. The books can be used from beginning level through intermediate level. They parallel the first three levels of basal series, and can be used as supplements to series or as stand-alone skills texts. A unique feature of *Journeys* is that the books can be used to construct a curriculum in those cases where student skills are at different levels. That is, in those classes where reading ability is at a higher level than speaking ability, the teacher is free to choose texts at appropriate levels. Each book can be used separately.

Journeys can be used with high school-aged students and up.

Journeys takes three notions very seriously:

1. Beginning level students have brains and hearts. They live in an interesting world that they are interested in.

2. Learning needs to be recycled. Rather than work on the same skill or topic across all four books during the same week, topics and language are recycled across the books to keep what students have learned active. Teachers who want to can teach the books out of order because the syllabus of each book progresses slowly.

3. It is possible for beginning level students to work with sophisticated content, yet complete simple tasks. In general, students can understand a much higher level of language than they can produce. By grading tasks, that is, keeping them simple at a beginning level, the linguistic demands made of the students are kept relatively low, but the content of the exercises remains interesting to adult learners.

Steven Brown

Youngstown State University

Acknowledgements

Interacting with people from other cultures and learning from those interactions have always been, for me, important parts of my "journeys." Often these interactions are "on the road," but as an English Language teacher, I am also fortunate that I can have these contacts on a daily basis--in my classroom, as I teach and learn from my students. My first acknowledgement goes to my students, the many hundreds of students, who have met me at different crossroads and added so much to my understanding of the world and appreciation of our human diversity and similarity. They have truly inspired me.

My heartfelt thanks also go to the many people who have left their mark on this book--colleagues, editors, artists, researchers. I especially wish to extend my appreciation to Nancy Baxer of Prentice Hall Asia for her enthusiasm. Her dedication to this "journey" continued unabated even when roads seemed impassable.

Finally, my thanks go to my family and friends for all that add to my "journeys." In particular, I am grateful for Michelle Rene-Ryan, for all that she gives: encouragement, food for thought, advice, laughter, support, understanding.

Roni Lebauer

Dedicated in loving memory to

my brother, Terry Lebauer

Work in groups of three. Look at the map. Can you name the countries (1 to 20) in your own language? Can you say them in English?

1. Australia	6. Japan	11. Taiwan	16. Vietnam
2. Mexico	7. Brazil	12. New Zealand	17. Saudi Arabia
3. Korea	8. Egypt	13. India	18. England
4. France	9. Canada	14. Chile	19. Guatemala
5. The USA	10. South Africa	15. The Philippines	20. Afghanistan

Try to number each country on the map. If you don't know, guess!

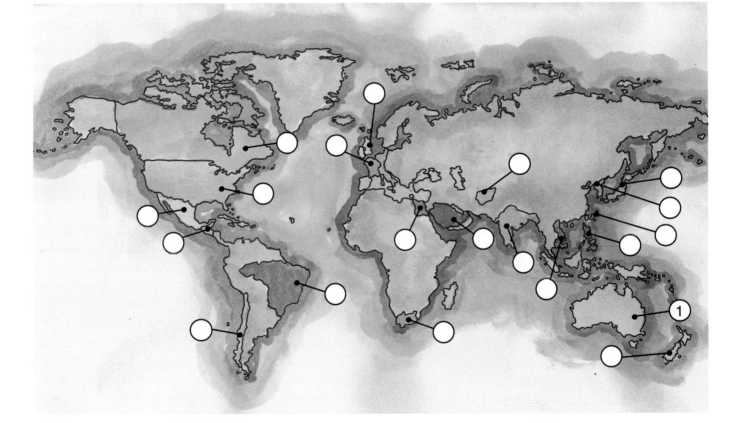

Talk with a classmate. Take turns asking and answering these questions.

1. What's your name? *My name is...*
2. Where are you from? *I'm from...*
3. Do you live in a big city, a small city, a town, or the country? *I live in...*

READING 1.1

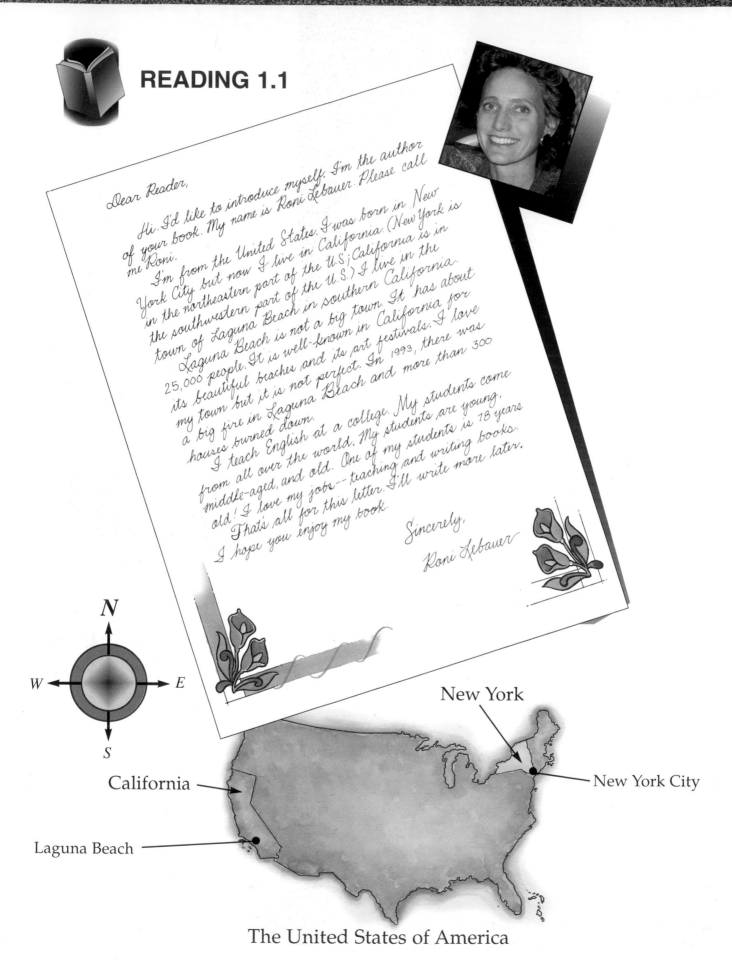

Dear Reader,

Hi. I'd like to introduce myself. I'm the author of your book. My name is Roni Lebauer. Please call me Roni.

I'm from the United States. I was born in New York City but now I live in California. (New York is in the northeastern part of the U.S.; California is in the southwestern part of the U.S.) I live in the town of Laguna Beach in southern California.

Laguna Beach is not a big town. It has about 25,000 people. It is well-known in California for its beautiful beaches and its art festivals. I love my town but it is not perfect. In 1993, there was a big fire in Laguna Beach and more than 300 houses burned down.

I teach English at a college. My students come from all over the world. My students are young, middle-aged, and old. One of my students is 18 years old! I love my jobs -- teaching and writing books.

That's all for this letter. I'll write more later. I hope you enjoy my book.

Sincerely,

Roni Lebauer

N
W E
S

California

Laguna Beach

New York

New York City

The United States of America

UNDERSTANDING

Check (√) the correct picture or pictures.

1. Roni's town

☐   ☑   ☐

2. Roni's class

☐   ☐   ☐

3. Laguna Beach is well-known in California for its _____.

☐   ☐   ☐

4. In 1993, there was a _____ in Laguna Beach.

☐   ☐   ☐

VOCABULARY

Read the information. Then, number the Australian cities on the map.

1. Melbourne is on the southeastern coast of Australia.
2. Perth is on the southwestern coast of Australia.
3. Cairns is on the northeastern coast of Australia.
4. Brisbane is on the eastern coast of Australia.
5. Darwin is on the northern coast of Australia.

READING 1.2

Look quickly at five of Roni's student records.

Last Name _Chen_
First Name _Shu Ling_
Middle Name _____

Birthplace _Taipei, Taiwan_
Nationality _Taiwanese_

Native Language(s) _Chinese_
Age _27_

Last Name _Park_
First Name _In Sook_
Middle Name _____

Birthplace _Pusan, South Korea_
Nationality _Korean_

Native Language(s) _Korean_
Age _18_

Last Name _Nguyen_
First Name _Cuong_
Middle Name _____

Birthplace _Hue, Vietnam_
Nationality _Vietnamese_

Native Language(s) _Vietnamese and Chinese_
Age _19_

Last Name _Oda_
First Name _Meyumi_
Middle Name _____

Birthplace _Sao Paulo, Brazil_
Nationality _Japanese_

Native Language(s) _Japanese and Portuguese_
Age _42_

Last Name _Taleb_
First Name _Omar_
Middle Name _Mohammed_

Birthplace _Alexandria, Egypt_
Nationality _Egyptian_

Native Language(s) _Arabic_
Age _78_

SCANNING

How many questions can you answer in two minutes? Write *T* if the sentence is true; write *F* if the sentence is false.

<u>F</u>   **1.** Ms. Chen is 25 years old.
___   **2.** Miss Park is from North Korea.
___   **3.** Megumi Oda was born in Brazil.
___   **4.** Miss Park is 18 years old.
___   **5.** Mr. Taleb's first name is Mohammed.
___   **6.** Mr. Taleb is from Saudi Arabia.
___   **7.** Ms. Chen was born in Japan.
___   **8.** Omar Taleb's native language is Arabic.

___   **9.** Shu Ling's first name is Chen.
___   **10.** Mr. Nguyen is from Hanoi, Vietnam.
___   **11.** Cuong is a teenager.
___   **12.** Mr. Taleb is a young man.
___   **13.** Megumi Oda speaks Portuguese.
___   **14.** Megumi is 24 years old.
___   **15.** Mr. Nguyen speaks Chinese.

THINK ABOUT IT

1. Which student is from Africa? _____
2. Which students are from Asia? _____ ,
_____ , and _____ .
3. Which student is from South America? _____

DO IT

Write the students' names in alphabetical order. Write the family name first.

1. Chen, Shu Ling
2.
3.
4.
5.

BEFORE READING 1.3

Look at the title and the picture. What do you think this article will be about?
Check (√) your guess.

_____	a small building	_____	a small person
_____	a small country	_____	a small amount of money

Read the first sentence of the story. Was your guess right? Now what do you think this
article will tell about this small country? Check (√) your guesses.

_____	the number of people	_____	the location
_____	the languages that people speak	_____	the food that people eat
_____	the religion of the people	_____	the size
_____	the number of schools	_____	the government
_____	the number of cars		

READING 1.3

Small... but not the smallest!

France

Mediterranean
Sea

M _ _ _ _ _

1   It's not hard to walk around this country in an hour or two. It's only
six-tenths of a square mile (one square kilometer)! It's a small country, but
it's not the smallest in the world.

  Do you know the name of the country? It borders
5 France on 3 sides. If you walk to the east, you come to
France. If you walk to the west, you come to France
again! If you walk to the north, you come to... France
again! If you walk to the south, however, you don't
come to France. You come to the Mediterranean coast
10 and the Mediterranean Sea.

  Do you know the name of this country yet?

  The population is about 30,000 and the people
speak French. Most of its people are Roman Catholic.

  Do you know the name now?

15 The government is a monarchy. This means there is
a royal family with a king or queen or prince or
princess. The present leader is Prince Rainier III.

  Do you know the name now?

  This country is well-known for its beauty and
20 its gambling casinos.

  Now, do you know? It's Monaco!

AFTER READING 1.3

1. Look back at your guesses on page 6. Were you correct?

2. A different title for this article could be

___ Gambling   ___ Prince Rainier III   ___ Roman Catholics   ___ Monaco

3. Match the information about Monaco.

1. Size	a. Prince Rainier III
2. Location	b. Six-tenths of a square mile (1 square kilometer)
3. Population	c. French
4. Language	d. monarchy
5. Religion	e. Roman Catholic
6. Kind of government	f. about 30,000
7. Present leader	g. France is on its north, east, and west borders. The Mediterranean Sea is to the south.

LOOKING AT WORDS

When you read, sometimes you don't know a word. Sometimes you need to stop and look up the word in a dictionary. Other times, you can guess from the information around the word. Look at this example from the reading.

It *borders* France on 3 sides. If you walk to the east, you come to France. If you walk to the west, you come to France again! If you walk to the north, you come to...France again! If you walk to the south, however, you don't come to France.

You don't need to look up the word *borders* in a dictionary. You can guess. What do you think the verb *border* means?

_____

 **CHALLENGE**

How much do you know about other countries? Try to answer these questions. If you get seven or more right answers, you know a lot !

1. **Which city is the capital of India?**
   a. New Delhi   b. Kabul   c. Bombay   d. Kathmandu

2. **Which city has the largest population?**
   a. Sao Paulo, Brazil   b. Seoul, South Korea   c. New York, U. S. A.
   d. Mexico City, Mexico

3. **Which country is a monarchy?**
   a. Egypt   b. Spain   c. Mexico   d. Vietnam

4. **Which country is in Africa?**
   a. Jordan   b. Kuwait   c. Nigeria   d. Afghanistan

5. **Which country is in South America?**
   a. Chile   b. Guatemala   c. Canada   d. Togo

6. **Which country borders Vietnam?**
   a. Thailand   b. Malaysia   c. Japan   d. China

7. **Which country has no coast?**
   a. Afghanistan   b. Indonesia   c. France   d. Algeria

8. **Where is Mount Everest, the highest mountain in the world?**
   a. Tanzania   b. Nepal   c. France   d. The United States

9. **How many countries are there in Africa?**
   a. 5-10   b. 11-19   c. 20-29   d. More than 30

10. **Which country has the largest population?**
    a. India   b. The United States   c. China   d. Indonesia

QUOTES AND SAYINGS ABOUT THE WORLD	• *We are citizens of the world.* • *It's a small world.*

Check (√) the picture of the language classroom that you like best for studying. Tell your classmates your choice.

Talk with a classmate. Take turns asking and answering these questions.

1. Do you like large, medium-size, or small language classes?
2. How many students do you like in your language classes?
3. Do you use computers in your language classes? If "yes," do you like to use computers?
4. Do you work in groups in your language classes? If "yes," do you like to work in groups?

READING 2.1

Monday, Apri

The Herald

Survey: What Kind Of Teacher Do You Like?

Carolina Santos Age: 19 Country: Colombia	**Wong Yi Hwa** Age: 28 Country: Taiwan	**Han Suk Lee** Age: 42 Country: Korea	**Hideo Ogama** Age: 21 Country: Japan	**Stefan Rudsky** Age: 45 Country: Poland	**Anant Kasim** Age: 37 Country: Thailand
"I like a teacher who has a sense of humor. I like to laugh."	*"I like a teacher who knows the subject well. I like a teacher who can answer all my questions."*	*"I like a teacher who makes the class interesting. I don't like to feel bored."*	*"I like a teacher who gives easy tests. I don't like to study very much."*	*"I like a teacher who gives a lot of homework. I don't want to be lazy."*	*"I like a teacher who is patient with me when I don't understand the lesson."*

YOUR TURN

Which person do you agree with? What kind of teacher do you like?

I like a teacher who _____

_____

_____

_____

_____

UNDERSTANDING

Look at these drawings. Write the names of the students (from page 10) who like these kinds of teachers. (Sometimes two different answers are possible.)

1. _____

2. _____

3. _____

4. _____

VOCABULARY

Match the pictures with the descriptions.

1. Who is the teacher in Room #301? Where is he? The teacher isn't at his desk. The students aren't at their desks. Books and papers are all over the teacher's desk. The eraser is on the floor. The garbage can is full of paper.

2. Who is the teacher in Room #302? Where is she? The students are at their desks but the teacher isn't there. Each student is ready with a pen, a piece of paper, and an open book, but there is no teacher!

3. Where are the students in Room #303? The teacher is at the board. She has a piece of chalk in her hand. The homework assignment is on the board. She has one book on her desk. The clock says 9:00. Why aren't the students there?

4. Look at Room #304. It looks perfect. The teacher is at his desk. The students are in their seats. Each student has a notebook and pen. The clock says 9:00 and they are ready to work.

a.

b.

c.

d.

READING 2.2

Ivana and Ayako just registered for their classes at college.
Look at their registration receipts.

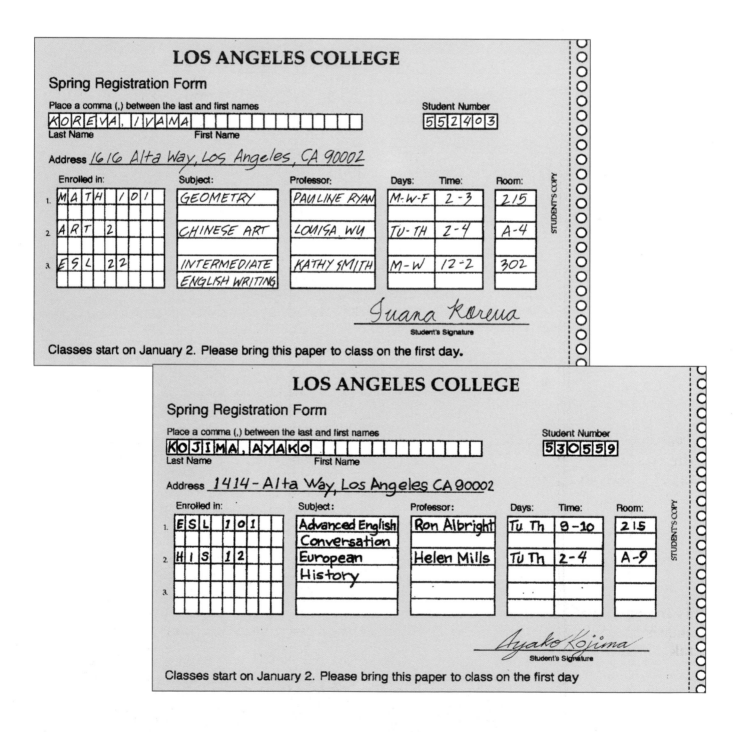

LOS ANGELES COLLEGE

Spring Registration Form

Place a comma (,) between the last and first names

K O R E V A , I V A N A   Student Number: 5 5 2 4 0 3

Last Name   First Name

Address: 1616 Alta Way, Los Angeles, CA 90002

Enrolled in:	Subject:	Professor:	Days:	Time:	Room:
1. MATH 101	GEOMETRY	PAULINE RYAN	M-W-F	2-3	215
2. ART 2	CHINESE ART	LOUISA WU	TU-TH	2-4	A-4
3. ESL 22	INTERMEDIATE ENGLISH WRITING	KATHY SMITH	M-W	12-2	302

Juana Korewa
Student's Signature

STUDENT'S COPY

Classes start on January 2. Please bring this paper to class on the first day.

LOS ANGELES COLLEGE

Spring Registration Form

Place a comma (,) between the last and first names

K O J I M A , A Y A K O   Student Number: 5 3 0 5 5 9

Last Name   First Name

Address: 1414 - Alta Way, Los Angeles CA 90002

Enrolled in:	Subject:	Professor:	Days:	Time:	Room:
1. ESL 101	Advanced English Conversation	Ron Albright	Tu Th	9-10	215
2. HIS 12	European History	Helen Mills	Tu Th	2-4	A-9
3.					

Ayako Kojima
Student's Signature

STUDENT'S COPY

Classes start on January 2. Please bring this paper to class on the first day

SCANNING

How many questions can you answer in two minutes? Write *T* if the sentence is true; write *F* if the sentence is false.

T   1. Ivana is registered for 3 classes.

___ 2. Ivana's student number is 592403.

___ 3. Ayako is registered for an art class.

___ 4. Ivana's last name is Koreva.

___ 5. Math 101 meets in room 200.

___ 6. Ayako is registered for Beginning English Conversation.

___ 7. Math 101 meets on Mondays and Wednesdays and Fridays.

___ 8. The teacher for Math 101 is Pauline Ryan.

___ 9. Ayako's last name is Kojima.

___ 10. Ivana is registered for Advanced English Writing.

___ 11. Ayako is registered for 2 classes.

___ 12. Ayako's classes are on Tuesdays and Thursdays.

___ 13. European History meets 3 days every week.

___ 14. Ayako's student number is 530559.

___ 15. European History meets in room 215.

THINK ABOUT IT

Ivana and Ayako want to take a psychology class together but they don't want to drop the classes they already have. There are three sections of the class. Which one can they take? Circle your choice.

Psychology 1: Introduction to Psychology	
Section 1	Tu Th 9 - 10:30
Section 2	M W 1:30 - 3
Section 3	Tu Th 12 - 1:30

Ivana and Ayako want to take a biology class together but they don't want to drop the classes they already have. There are three sections of the class. Which one can they take? Circle your choice.

Biology 1: Introduction to Biology	
Section 1	M W F 12 - 1:30
Section 2	Tu Th 1:30 - 3
Section 3	F 10 - 11:30

BEFORE READING 2.3

Before reading, look at the title and the picture. What do you think this article will be about? Check (√) your guess.

___ the number of years teachers study in different countries

___ the number of days students attend school every year in different countries

___ the subjects students study in different countries

___ the number of years students attend school in different countries

READING 2.3

The School Year

1 How many days per week are schools open in your country? How many long vacations do students have? Is it good to have a long summer or winter vacation? Do students 5 learn important real-life lessons outside of school during long vacations? Do they get a healthy rest? Or do students forget a lot when they have a long vacation away from school?

Many educators are talking about these 10 questions. In the United States, students attend an average of 180 days of school per school year. This is the same as Sweden and Mexico. In Canada, students attend an average of 195 to 200 days per year. In South Korea, students attend an average of 220 15 days per year. Topping the list is Japan where students attend schools 228 days per year.

What is best? Most studies show that students learn more when they spend more time in class. Studies also show that many 20 students forget school lessons during long vacations.

However, not everyone likes the idea of a long school year. Children and parents sometimes want more time together. 25 Students want time to relax. Some schools say that a longer school year is too expensive.

What do you think?

AFTER READING 2.3

1. Look back at your guess on page 14. Were you correct?
2. This reading gives examples of different school years in different countries. Can you put the information in a chart?

Countries	Average Number of School days per year
United States	*180 days*

3. Which are reasons for a longer school year? Check (√) your answers.

___ 1. Students forget their lessons during long vacations.

___ 2. Students need to relax.

___ 3. Parents and children need to spend time together.

___ 4. Students learn more when the school year is longer.

___ 5. Keeping schools open for a longer time can be expensive.

LOOKING AT WORDS

A. Look at the word *educator*. An educator is a person who educates students. The ending *or* or *er* means "a person who does something." Can you think of three other words that end in *or* or *er*?

_____   _____   _____

B. Swedish students attend an average of 180 days of school *per year*. This means that Swedish students attend 180 days of school out of 365 days (in a year). Complete the following sentences with a time expression and the word *per*.

1. Japanese students attend school Monday, Tuesday, Wednesday, Thursday, Friday, and Saturday. They attend school six days __*per*__ __*week*__.
2. American students have vacations in July and August. They have vacations two months _____ _____. They attend school _____ _____ _____ year.
3. Joao studies every night from 6 p.m. to 8 p.m. He studies _____ _____ _____ day.
4. How many hours do you study English per day? I study English _____ _____ _____ day.
5. How many days per week do you go to school? I go to school _____ _____ _____ week.

CHALLENGE

There are 5 students: Millie, Malka, Sima, Boris, and James. They each have a different last name: Anders, Monroe, Barak, Wu, or Odeh. They each have a different favorite subject: art, psychology, English, math, or history. Read the clues. Can you figure out the students' last names and their favorite subjects?

Hint: Pay attention to the words "Mr.," "Mrs.," and "Ms."

Clues

1. Millie, Malka, and Sima are women. Boris and James are men.
2. Boris' last name is Anders.
3. Mr. Monroe's favorite subject is psychology.
4. Millie doesn't like history or math or art.
5. Ms. Barak's favorite subject is art.
6. Sima hates art.
7. Ms. Odeh's favorite subject is history.
8. Mrs. Wu and Sima drive to school together.

First Name	Last Name	Favorite Subject
Millie		
Malka		
Sima		
Boris		
James		

QUOTES AND SAYINGS ABOUT EDUCATION AND LEARNING	• *I hear and I forget. I see and I remember. I do and I understand.* • *Experience is the best teacher.*

Look at these pictures of different family members.
Complete the sentences saying who the people in the pictures are.

Maybe they are _husband and wife_.
Maybe they are _brother and sister_.

Maybe they are _____.
Maybe they are _____.

Maybe they are _____.
Maybe they are _____.

Maybe they are _____.
Maybe they are _____.

Talk with a classmate. Take turns asking and answering these questions.

1. Who do you live with?
2. How many brothers and sisters do you have?
3. Do you have any children? How many? Are they boys or girls? How old are they?
4. What is a good number of children to have, in your opinion?

READING 3.1

Dear Ana,

I'm a little sad today. It's Mother's Day but I can't see my mother. I can talk to her on the phone but that's all.

What's the problem? The problem is that I live on the west coast of the U.S. and my parents live on the southeast coast of the U.S. in Florida. There are more than 2000 miles (about 3300 kilometers) between us.

My parents are retired. They are both in their sixties and -- I am happy to say -- very healthy. They love being retired. They have friends in their neighborhood. My father plays tennis. My mother swims.

They travel to California once a year and I travel to Florida to see them once or twice a year.

Usually, I don't feel sad about this. Most of the time, I like my independence. Maybe it's just because it's Mother's Day.

I hope you and your family are well.

Write soon,

Roni

Dear Roni,

Sometimes I wish I had your problem. As you know, I live with my parents. I'm 27 and they always want to tell me how to live my life. If I come home late, they ask me many questions: who? what? where? why? If I look sad, they ask me many questions: who? what? when? where? why? Sometimes, I don't want to answer.

I know they love me and I love them, but sometimes I want some independence.

Nothing is perfect.

Best wishes,
Ana

UNDERSTANDING

Check (√) the answer or answers.

1. Roni feels _____.

2. Where is Florida?

3. Roni and her mother can _____ together on Mother's Day.

4. What do Roni's parents do in Florida?

5. What is Ana's problem?

6. How often do Roni's parents travel to California?

_____ one time per year   _____ two times per year

_____ one or two times per year   _____ on Mother's Day

READING 3.2

Read these newspaper announcements.

Society News

BIRTHS

Born to Bob and Toni Kang, at Cedar Medical Center, on March 2, a son, Wallace James.

Born to Eric Butler and Melissa Henderson, at Oakwood Hospital, on March 11, a daughter, Sarah Joanne.

Born to Ken and Miyuki Mori, at Cedar Medical Center, on March 14, twin girls, Ami and Rika.

MARRIAGES

Julio and Naomi Ruiz of Los Angeles, California, are pleased to announce the marriage of their daughter, Ana Beatriz, to James Bailey Jr., son of Mr. and Mrs. James Bailey of San Francisco, California.

The wedding will take place at Lake Forest Church on Saturday, March 30 at 11 a.m. A reception will follow at the home of the bride's aunt, Ms. Mercedes Ruiz.

DEATHS

Donna Jean Bryant died Tuesday, March 22 at her London home. She was 84.

She is survived by her husband, James Bryant; her daughter, Elaine Lee; her son-in-law, Richard Lee; her grandson, Steven Lee; her brother, Carl Stone and her sister in law, Lisa Stone, and 5 nieces and nephews.

Peter Rivera, a native of Miami, Florida died on Friday.

VOCABULARY

bride	*n.*	the woman who is getting married
groom	*n.*	the man who is getting married
reception	*n.*	a large party (often after a wedding ceremony)
twins	*n.*	two babies born together

Write *T* if the sentence is true; write *F* if the sentence is false.

<u>F</u>   **1.** Sara Joanne was born on March 4.

___   **2.** The Ruiz-Bailey wedding is on March 11.

___   **3.** The Ruiz-Bailey wedding is at Lake Forest Church.

___   **4.** Ken and Miyuki Mori had twin boys.

___   **5.** The Kangs had a son named James Wallace.

___   **6.** Sarah Joanne was born at Cedar Medical Center.

___   **7.** Donna Jean Bryant died on March 22.

___   **8.** Donna Jean Bryant was married.

___   **9.** Donna Jean Bryant had no grandchildren.

___ **10.** Donna Jean Bryant had a son.

___ **11.** The new husband and wife are Julio and Naomi Ruiz.

___ **12.** The groom's parents live in Los Angeles.

___ **13.** The bride's parents live in Los Angeles.

___ **14.** Donna Jean Bryant was 84 when she died.

___ **15.** Donna Jean Bryant died in Los Angeles.

DO IT

Circle all the family relationship words (for example, *mother, father, brother,* etc) in the birth, marriage, and death announcements on page 20.

Example:

> Born to Bob and Toni Kang, at Cedar Medical Center, on March 2, a (son,) Wallace James.

THINK ABOUT IT

Are there birth, marriage, and death announcements in the newspapers you read? How are they the same or different from the ones on page 20?

BEFORE READING 3.3

Look at the title and the picture. What do you think this article will be about? Guess one idea. Check (√) your guess.

—— different kinds of houses

—— different kinds of families

—— one big house

—— one big family

READING 3.3

A Full House

1   **C**amille and Mike Geraldi are married and live with their children near Miami, Florida in the U. S. A. Mike is a doctor. Camille is a housewife and former nurse. They sound like
5 an average family. In some ways they are but in many ways, they are not.

   The average family in the U. S. has two or three children. The Geraldis have seventeen children. That is not all. Fifteen of these
10 seventeen children are adopted children between the ages of one and nine. Each of the adopted children has a severe physical or mental disability.

   A day with the Geraldi family is not
15 average. Camille wakes up before dawn. She and three helpers wake, wash, dress, and feed the seventeen children. After breakfast, eleven of the children go to special schools. At 7:30, Camille takes a nap for two hours. When she
20 wakes up at 9:30, she starts doing the laundry. During the day, she feeds and plays with the children. Camille cooks dinner before Mike comes home from work. Mike cleans up after dinner.
25   Camille is busy even at night. She often wakes up to take care of the children who need her. She almost never has a full night's sleep.

   Camille and Mike try to plan time for each other. Every Wednesday, they have a lunch "date" and every other Saturday, they go away by themselves 30 for the day.

   Camille says, "It fulfills me to help these children. It's a need I have." Camille loves her life. She looks at other people and thinks, "What a dull life they have."

   In many ways, the Geraldis are not an average 35 family. However, in some ways, they are. Like most families, they laugh and cry together and love each other a lot.

VOCABULARY

to adopt	*v.*	to take children who were born to other people and raise them as one's own
dull	*adj.*	boring
former	*adj.*	in the past
to fulfill	*v.*	to make happy and satisfied

AFTER READING 3.3

1. Look back at your guess on page 22. Was your guess correct?

2. A different title for this article could be
    a. Disabled Children
    b. Doctors and Nurses
    c. An Average Family?
    d. Life in the U.S.A.

3. What do the Geraldis do every day? Write 1 next to the first thing;
    write 2 next to the second thing, and so on.

    _1_ Mike comes home from work.
    _____ Camille gets up before dawn.
    _____ Mike cleans up after dinner.
    _____ Camille often gets up at night to take care of the children.
    _____ Some of the children go to special schools.
    _____ Camille and three helpers wake, wash, dress, and feed the seventeen children.
    _____ Camille takes a nap.
    _____ Camille starts doing the laundry; then, she feeds and plays with the children.

4. When do Mike and Camille see each other alone?_____

LOOKING AT WORDS

When you are reading and you don't know a word, you can try to guess from the information around the word. Look at the following example from the reading.

> Camille wakes up before *dawn*. She and three helpers wake, wash, dress, and feed the seventeen children. After breakfast, eleven of the children go to special schools. At 7:30, Camille *takes a nap* for two hours. When she wakes up at 9:30, she starts doing the laundry.

You can guess what the word *nap* means from the information in the story. What is your guess?

_____

If you can't guess and if you think the word is important, sometimes you can use a dictionary. In the dictionary, there are two definitions for *dawn*. One is for a noun (n.); one is for a verb (v.).

dawn (dôn) *n.* the time of day when light first appears before the sun rises

dawn (dôn) *v.* to begin to grow light immediately before the sun rises

What does the word *dawn* mean in the sentence *Camille wakes up before* dawn?

_____

CHALLENGE

Can you complete the crossword puzzle? All of the words are in Unit 3.

<u>Across</u>

3. My _____ is Roni.
4. Roni's parents do not work. They are _____.
7. I have no sisters but I have a _____.
10. She is tired so she takes a _____.
11. Mary's daughter has a son. This boy is Mary's _____.
12. Call me on the _____. My number is 555-6780.
13. A woman who is getting married is a _____.

<u>Down</u>

1. He is Carol's son. Carol is his _____.
2. She wants her freedom. She wants her _____.
5. I have some trouble. I have a _____.
6. A little girl was born to Alan and Sue Ryan. She is their _____.
8. Two people who were born at the same time to the same parents are _____.
9. _____ is the time when the sun starts rising.

QUOTES AND SAYINGS ABOUT FAMILIES	• *Like father, like son.* • *Like mother, like daughter.*

Look at these pictures of people at work. What are their jobs? Write the job name under each picture. Use each of the words in the box only once.

singer	mechanic	astronaut	bank teller
doctor	waiter	engineer	farmer

bank teller

Put *1* next to the job that you like best for yourself. Put *2* next to the job that you like second best. Put *3* next to the job that you like third best. Tell your classmates your choices.

I put 1 next to the picture of the _____ *because* _____.

I put 2 next to the picture of the _____ *because* _____.

I put 3 next to the picture of the _____ *because* _____.

Talk to a classmate. If your partner has a job, ask these questions.

1. What kind of work do you do?
2. Where do you work?
3. Is your work easy or hard? Interesting or boring?
4. Do you like your work? Why or why not?

If your partner doesn't have a job, ask these questions.

1. What kind of work do you want to do in the future?
2. Why do you want to do that kind of work?

READING 4.1

Survey: Do You Like Your Job?

Maria Biondi

"I work in a market. I hate my job. Every day, I look at 64 chickens that I have to clean. When I arrive at the market and see those chickens, I always sigh. I do the same thing every day--grab a chicken, cut it open, clean it, put it in the refrigerator--64 times. At the end of the day, I always feel sick from all the blood and smells. My fingers hurt because I wash the chickens in cold water. When I go home, I just want to close my eyes and rest."

"Do I like my job? Absolutely. I love kids. Every morning, I drive the same route to pick up the kids and take them to school. In the afternoon, I pick them up at school and take them home again. Sometimes, they're really noisy and it gives me a headache, but usually they are fun and friendly. I try to be a friend and parent to them. I ask them about their day, their schoolwork, and their grades."

Masayuki Miyata

Lily Wang

"I have an exciting job. I'm a reporter for a newspaper. My days are always different. I never know what will happen. I never know where I'll need to go. I never feel bored. Oh, excuse me. I've got to run. I have an interview with Meryl Streep, the actress, in 10 minutes."

UNDERSTANDING

Check (√) the information that is true for Maria, Masayuki, or Lily.

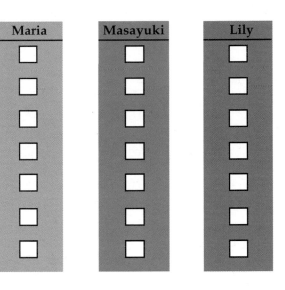

	Maria	Masayuki	Lily
1. Doesn't like their job.	☐	☐	☐
2. Goes someplace different every day.	☐	☐	☐
3. Works with children.	☐	☐	☐
4. Interviews famous people.	☐	☐	☐
5. Always feels sick at the end of the day.	☐	☐	☐
6. Drives every day.	☐	☐	☐
7. Sometimes gets a headache because of the noise.	☐	☐	☐

VOCABULARY

What jobs do these people have? Choose from the words in the box.

nurse
florist
accountant
secretary
fire fighter
teacher
mechanic
musician
salesperson
flight attendant
businessperson
plumber
computer programmer
reporter
waiter

1. I get up early to buy flowers from the market.
   Then, I sell the flowers in my store.
   I am a _____.

2. I work in a hospital but I'm not a doctor. I give
   patients their medicine and I take their temperature.
   I'm a _____.

3. People come to me when they have problems with
   their car. I find out what the problem is and I fix it..
   I'm a _____.

4. I play guitar in a band. We play at parties and clubs.
   I'm a _____.

5. I work for an airline. I help people on planes and
   serve food and drinks.
   I'm a _____.

READING 4.2

Zeno Inc. exports products from Taiwan. The company is looking for a secretary. They placed an ad in *The International Herald Tribune*.

SECRETARY *WANTED*

Immediate opening for experienced secretary. Must type 60+ wpm and have good phone skills. Must be organized and flexible. Must be fluent in French, Chinese, and English. Knowledge of computers helpful. Send resume to Zeno Inc., Box 2121 care of The International Herald Tribune.

...ust be v...
editing, proof
and the like. She
willing to work
must have total ...
plete devotion
work.

These requirem...
strict and any d...
from the re...
...lt in ...

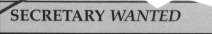

UNDERSTANDING

Check (√) the correct answer.

1. This is an <u>immediate opening</u>.
   ___ a. The job is open now and the company wants to hire someone as soon as possible.
   ___ b. Someone has the job now but in the future, the job may be open.

2. The secretary must type 60+ wpm. <u>Wpm</u> means
   ___ a. weeks per month.
   ___ b. words per minute.

3. The secretary must have <u>good phone skills</u>. The secretary must
   ___ a. sound nice on the phone.
   ___ b. take good messages when someone calls.
   ___ c. both a. and b.

4. The secretary must be <u>fluent</u> in French, Chinese, and English. The secretary must
   ___ a. speak these languages very well.
   ___ b. speak these languages a little.

5. Knowledge of computers is <u>helpful</u>. This means
   ___ a. the secretary must know about computers.
   ___ b. it is good if the secretary knows about computers but it isn't necessary.

Michael Chen and Anh Nguyen are interested in the job at Zeno Inc. Look at their resumes.

Michael Chen

17 Lexington
Toronto, Canada M4Y 1H5
Tel: 416-773-9231
Fax: 416-783-0295

Education: 1991-1992 St. Michael's Technical College,
Toronto, Canada

Experience: 1993-1994: Secretary
Soho Computers,Toronto, Canada

Skills: Keyboarding: 60 wpm.
Dictation: 100 wpm.
Computer Programs: Windows, Lotus, Excel,
PageMaker, etc.

Languages: Native Speaker of Chinese (Mandarin)
Fluent in English and French.
Fair Spanish

Please see attached references

Anh Nguyen

12 Rue du Mont
Paris, France 94110
Telephone: (331) 463 84 00

Work Experience: 1985-present:
Executive Secretary
Larousse Inc.,
Paris, France 1982-1985:
Receptionist, Tivoli Co.,
Paris, France

Office Skills: Typing: 80 wpm.
Familiar with various
computers and programs.
Fluent in Vietnamese, Chinese,
and French. Some English.

References are available upon request

Compare Michael Chen's and Anh Nguyen's skills. Write + to show who is better for the Zeno Inc. job at each skill. Write = to show they are the same.

	Michael Chen	Anh Nguyen
Typing		
Languages		
Computers		
Secretarial Experience		
Phone Skills		

THINK ABOUT IT

Who should get the job? Why?

CHALLENGE

Can you find 25 jobs in this puzzle? You may find the words vertically($\updownarrow$), horizontally ($\leftrightarrow$), or diagonally ($\nearrow$). Use the word list below.

actor	artist	baker	barber	butcher
cashier	carpenter	cook	dentist	doctor
engineer	farmer	florist	janitor	mechanic
nurse	painter	pilot	receptionist	reporter
secretary	tailor	teacher	teller	waiter

R	V	A	T	F	B	B	A	D	O	C	T	O	R	C	F	C
S	A	W	T	O	A	A	L	N	E	G	R	O	O	P	M	A
E	T	A	C	T	O	R	K	B	E	N	G	I	N	E	E	R
F	T	I	T	E	R	B	M	E	C	R	T	L	A	N	C	P
L	E	T	I	L	N	E	R	E	R	C	M	I	T	L	H	E
O	A	E	P	L	A	R	E	S	R	O	T	T	S	J	A	N
R	C	R	R	E	C	E	P	T	I	O	N	I	S	T	N	T
I	H	A	O	R	S	A	O	N	R	K	E	U	T	C	I	E
S	E	C	R	E	T	A	R	Y	L	Y	R	E	R	O	C	R
T	R	A	R	T	N	E	T	A	I	L	O	R	S	S	L	O
P	L	I	T	D	I	V	E	R	S	B	U	T	C	H	E	R
O	P	I	L	O	T	S	R	E	C	A	S	H	I	E	R	N
S	T	A	P	A	I	N	T	E	R	J	A	N	I	T	O	R

QUOTES AND SAYINGS ABOUT WORK	• *A woman's work is never done.*
	• *Many hands make light work.*

This is a folktale from Africa. It is a simple story but it has a deep meaning. What does it mean?

Friends

1 It's a beautiful day and a little frog is hopping in and out of the lake happily.

Suddenly, she sees something behind a rock. It's long and thin. Its skin is shiny with many colors.

"Hello," calls the little frog. "What are you doing behind the rock?"

5 "Just warming myself in the sun," answers the animal, a baby snake.

"Would you like to play with me?" asks the little frog.

The baby snake smiles (if snakes can smile) and moves in front of the rock.

The little frog and the baby snake play all day long. The little frog teaches the baby snake how to hop and the baby snake teaches the little frog how to climb
10 a tree.

At the end of the day, the two animals feel hungry and need to go home to eat. Before they say goodbye, they promise to return to the same lake and play together again.

"Thanks for teaching me how to hop," says the baby snake.

15 "Thanks for teaching me how to climb a tree," says the little frog.

When the little frog gets home, she shows her parents that she can climb a tree.

The frog's parents are very upset and angry. They ask, "How do you know that?"

"I learned from the baby snake. He's my new friend," says the little frog.

"Don't play with the baby snake again. We don't like the snake family.
20 They have poison in their teeth. We don't want to see you playing together again. And we don't want to see you climbing trees again. Do you understand?"

33

When the baby snake gets home, he shows his parents that he can hop.

The snake's parents are also very upset and angry. They ask, "How do you know how to hop?"

25 "I learned from the little frog. She's my new friend," says the baby snake.

"Don't play with the little frog again. We don't like the frog family. If you see the little frog again, catch him and eat him. That's what snakes do. And we don't want to see you hopping again. Do you understand?"

The next morning, the little frog and the baby snake go to the lake. But they don't go near 30 each other.

The little frog says (from far away), "I'm sorry. I can't climb with you today." The baby snake doesn't say anything. He thinks about his parents' words but he doesn't want to catch and eat the little frog. The baby snake just sighs and goes away.

From that day on, the little frog and the baby snake never play together again. But they often 35 sit alone in the sun and think about their one day of friendship.

UNDERSTANDING

Number the pictures in the correct order.

Look at these pictures of different foods. Check (√) the food(s) that you like to eat for lunch.

 steak

 rice

 French fries

 hamburger

 sandwich

 fish

 salad

 bread

 fruit

 ice cream

 cake

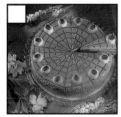 pizza

 chicken

 noodles

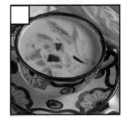 soup

Talk with a classmate. Take turns asking and answering these questions.

1. What do you like to eat for lunch?
2. What do you like to eat in the morning?
3. What do you like to drink in the morning?
4. Do you like to eat in restaurants?
5. How often do you eat in restaurants?
6. What is your favorite restaurant?

READING 6.1

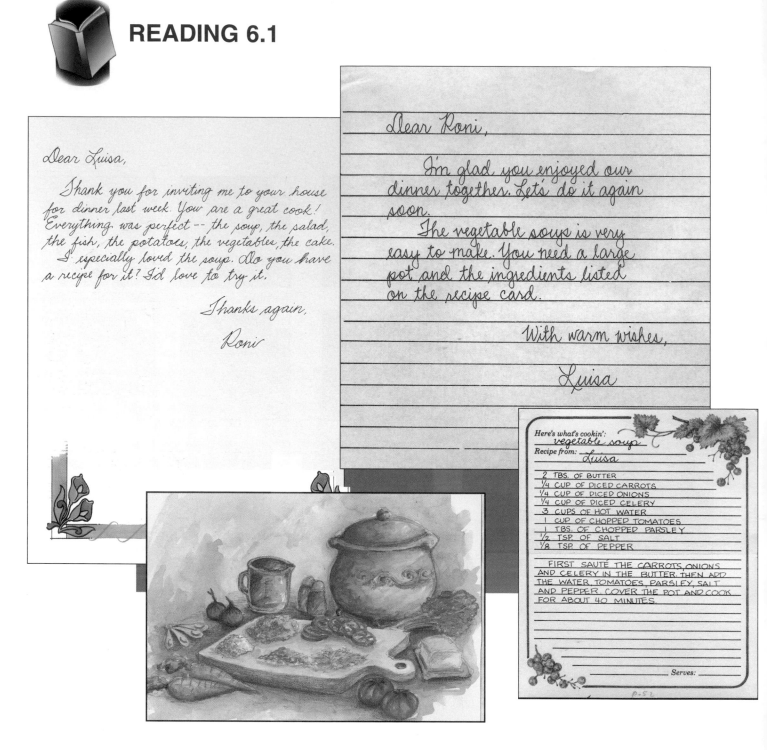

Dear Luisa,

Thank you for inviting me to your house for dinner last week. You are a great cook! Everything was perfect -- the soup, the salad, the fish, the potatoes, the vegetables, the cake.

I especially loved the soup. Do you have a recipe for it? I'd love to try it.

Thanks again,

Roni

Dear Roni,

I'm glad you enjoyed our dinner together. Let's do it again soon.

The vegetable soup is very easy to make. You need a large pot and the ingredients listed on the recipe card.

With warm wishes,

Luisa

Here's what's cookin':
vegetable soup
Recipe from: Luisa

2 TBS. OF BUTTER
1/4 CUP OF DICED CARROTS
1/4 CUP OF DICED ONIONS
1/4 CUP OF DICED CELERY
3 CUPS OF HOT WATER
1 CUP OF CHOPPED TOMATOES
1 TBS. OF CHOPPED PARSLEY
1/2 TSP. OF SALT
1/8 TSP. OF PEPPER

FIRST SAUTÉ THE CARROTS, ONIONS AND CELERY IN THE BUTTER. THEN ADD THE WATER, TOMATOES, PARSLEY, SALT AND PEPPER. COVER THE POT AND COOK FOR ABOUT 40 MINUTES.

Serves:

VOCABULARY FOR RECIPES

to chop	*v.*	to cut in small pieces
to dice	*v.*	to cut into small squares
to saute	*v.*	to cook quickly in hot oil or butter
tbs.	*n.*	tablespoon
tsp.	*n.*	teaspoon

UNDERSTANDING

1. Check (√) the food that Luisa cooked for dinner last week.

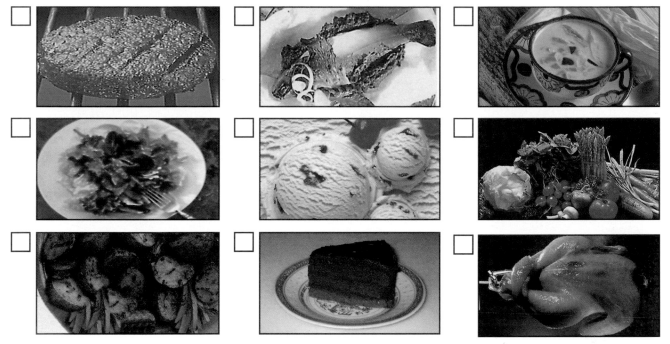

2. Number the pictures in the correct order to make Luisa's vegetable soup.

VOCABULARY

Complete the following sentences. Use the words in the box.

1. This vegetable is orange. It's a _____.
2. This fruit is yellow and sour. It's a _____.
3. This vegetable is light green. It's _____.
4. This fruit is yellow or pink. It has a lot of vitamin C.
   It's a _____.
5. This fruit is small and red. It has a pit. It's a _____.
6. This fruit is big. It is green on the outside and red on the inside.
   It has little black seeds. It's a _____.
7. This vegetable is light brown on the outside and white on the
   inside. When you cut it, you may cry. It's an _____.

| onion |
| cherry |
| grapefruit |
| celery |
| watermelon |
| banana |
| carrot |
| lemon |

JUST FOR FUN

EATS   by oldden

READING 6.2

Rudy's Restaurant

Soups

Chicken...	cup	1.50
	bowl	2.50
Vegetable..	cup	1.25
	bowl	2.25

Sandwiches
(served with French fries)

Chicken	4.75
Tuna fish	4.00
Cheese	3.50

Hamburgers
(served with French fries)

Plain	4.25
Cheeseburger	4.50

Small green salad	2.00
Large green salad	3.00

"Fast... and tasty!"

Desserts

Apple pie	2.50
Ice cream	1.50

Beverages

Coffee	.75
Tea	.75
Soda	1.00
Milk	1.00
Bottled water	1.00

Open 24 hours.
"We never sleep!"

SCANNING

How many questions can you answer in two minutes?

1. How much is a bowl of chicken soup? _____
2. How much is a large green salad? _____
3. How much is a plain hamburger? _____
4. How much is a glass of milk? _____
5. How many hours per day is Rudy's open? _____
6. I want a cheese sandwich and a cup of tea. How much is my bill? _____
7. How much is apple pie? _____
8. I want a small green salad and a chicken sandwich. How much is my bill? _____
9. How much is a cheeseburger? _____
10. How much is a cup of vegetable soup? _____
11. How much is a cup of coffee? _____
12. I want apple pie and ice cream. How much is my bill? _____

THINK ABOUT IT

Joon ordered a sandwich, a beverage, and a dessert at Rudy's Restaurant. His bill was $6.25. What did he order?

Gina ordered soup, a salad, and a beverage at Rudy's Restaurant. Her bill was $6.25. What did she order?

DO IT

Work with a partner. Use the menu on page 38. Ask what your partner would like to eat and drink. Write your partner's order and add up the bill. Then change roles.

Rudy's Restaurant	Order form no. 24
1. _____	_____
2. _____	_____
3. _____	_____
4. _____	_____
5. _____	
Total	_____

BEFORE READING 6.3

Talk with a classmate. Take turns asking "Do you think your diet is healthy? Why or why not?" Answer using these words: *always, often, sometimes, seldom, rarely, never.*

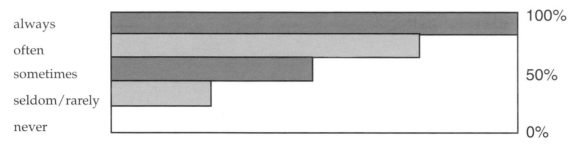

always	100%
often	
sometimes	50%
seldom/rarely	
never	0%

Example: I never drink coffee.

READING 6.3

Is Your Diet Healthy?

Are you eating right? Is your diet healthy or unhealthy? Are you getting the necessary vitamins? Are you eating too much fat? Are you eating enough fruit and vegetables? Take this quiz to find out. Write *yes* or *no*.

_____ 1. Do you rarely add butter or margarine to foods?

_____ 2. Do you eat fried foods less than twice a week?

_____ 3. Do you drink only low-fat milk (or no milk) and seldom eat high-fat cheese?

_____ 4. Do you seldom eat high-fat snack foods (such as potato chips)?

_____ 5. Do you seldom eat high-fat baked goods such as pies, cookies, and doughnuts?

_____ 6. Do you cut the fat from red meat and eat chicken without the skin?

_____ 7. Do you seldom eat bacon, hot dogs, and ham?

_____ 8. Do you eat wholegrain breads and pasta, brown rice or wholegrain cereal every day?

_____ 9. Do you often eat foods rich in vitamin C (such as oranges and grapefruits)?

_____ 10. Do you often eat dark green or deep yellow fruits and vegetables?

_____ 11. Do you often eat vegetables of the cabbage family, including broccoli, cabbage, cauliflower, or Brussels sprouts?

_____ 12. Do you rarely eat chocolate?

How many "yes" answers do you have? _____

- Zero to four "yes" answers means your diet is probably too high in fat and too low in fiber. You should start eating less fat and more fruit and vegetables.
- Five to eight "yes" answers means your diet is OK but it could be better. Try to reduce the fat and increase the fiber in your diet.
- Nine or more "yes" answers means your diet is great!

AFTER READING 6.3

Look at the survey on page 40 again.

1. Question 2 asks about fried foods. What fried foods do you eat?
   _____

2. Questions 4 and 5 ask about high-fat snack foods and baked goods. What high-fat snackfoods and baked goods do you eat? _____

3. Question 9 asks about foods rich in vitamin C. What foods rich in vitamin C do you eat?
   _____

4. Question 10 asks about dark green and deep yellow fruits and vegetables. What dark green and deep yellow fruits and vegetables do you eat? _____

5. Question 11 asks about vegetables of the cabbage family. What vegetables of the cabbage family do you eat? _____
   _____

6. How can you improve your diet? Write 2 more sentences with *should*.
   I should eat more dark green vegetables. _____
   _____
   _____

LOOKING AT WORDS

*H*ealthy means "good for our body and health." The prefix *un*-means "not." What does *unhealthy* mean? _____

The opposite of happy is _____.

The opposite of afraid is _____.

The opposite of comfortable is _____.

The opposite of lucky is _____.

CHALLENGE

Do you like chocolate? How much do you know about it? Answer the following questions about chocolate. Work with a partner, if you like. If you get seven or more correct, give yourself a "pat on the back" ... or a piece of chocolate!

True or False?

1. _____ Americans eat more chocolate on average than any other national group.

2. _____ The Aztec Indians of Mexico were the first to use cocoa.

3. _____ When the Aztecs made chocolate into a drink, they added hot red peppers to it.

4. _____ The word *chocolate* comes from an Aztec word, *xocaolatl*, which means "bitter water".

5. _____ People made chocolate into a drink before they made it into a candy.

6. _____ The Swiss were the first to add sugar to chocolate drinks.

7. _____ An English company made the first chocolate candy.

8. _____ People loved chocolate candies in the 1600s.

9. _____ People in the United Kingdom eat an average of 4.4 pounds (2 kilograms) of chocolate per year.

10. _____ Chocolate candy is rich in vitamin C and low in fat.

QUOTES AND SAYINGS ABOUT FOOD	• *Don't put all your eggs in one basket.* • *Man does not live by bread alone.*

Imagine: You see a $500 bill on the street. You pick it up.

 Check (√) the first place you will go with that money. Tell your classmates your choice.

 Talk with a classmate. Take turns asking and answering these questions.

1. Where do you shop for food?
2. Where do you shop for clothes?
3. Besides food and clothes, what do you often buy in stores?

READING 7.1

Survey: Do You Like To Shop?

Hanai Torii
Age: 42
Country: Japan

"Do I like to shop? Do children like ice cream? Of course! Whenever I have free time, I go shopping. There's always something fun to buy--shoes, clothes, make-up. Some might say I'm a 'shopaholic'!"

Lisa Bowers
Age: 38
Country: U. S.

"I'm always shopping. Jamie, my two-year- old, needs clothes or shoes. Sheri, my five-year-old needs things for school. The washing machine is broken. I need to look for another one. Do I ever shop for myself? Who has time? Is it fun? No way!"

Marco Luna
Age: 17
Country: Mexico

"I don't care about clothes and luckily, I don't need to shop for my food. The only kind of shopping I do is music shopping... and I love that! Hey... there's a Ruben Blades CD I don't have... and I hear that Madonna is coming out with a new one. It's a good thing I have a part-time job!"

Faridah Mohd Rani
Age: 62
Country: Indonesia

"I've got five grandchildren. I'm always looking for little things that I can buy them--a book, a shirt, a toy. I enjoy seeing their happiness. Perhaps I spoil them a little... but isn't that what grandmothers are for?"

Fernando Ramos
Age: 73
Country:
The Philippines

"At my age, I want to enjoy life. To me, shopping is a necessity, not a pleasure. I would rather take a walk and enjoy the sunshine, or visit and talk with friends. I only shop when I have to."

Jean Rene
Age: 37
Country: Canada

"Times are tough. My rent is high. Food is expensive. Clothes are expensive. I can't find a good job. Do I like to shop? What do you think? I feel sad and angry every time I walk into a store."

YOUR TURN

What about you? Do you like to shop?

UNDERSTANDING

Check (√) the correct box or boxes.

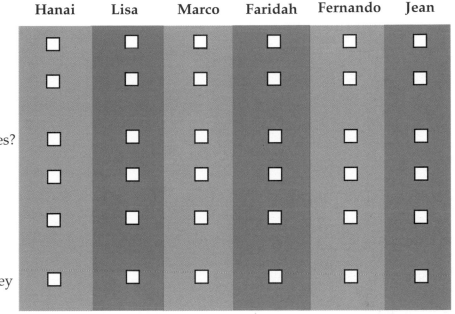

	Hanai	Lisa	Marco	Faridah	Fernando	Jean
1. Who likes to shop for clothes?	☐	☐	☐	☐	☐	☐
2. Who likes to buy things for herself or himself?	☐	☐	☐	☐	☐	☐
3. Who likes to go into music stores?	☐	☐	☐	☐	☐	☐
4. Who doesn't like shopping?	☐	☐	☐	☐	☐	☐
5. Who buys things for other people?	☐	☐	☐	☐	☐	☐
6. Who doesn't have enough money to shop?	☐	☐	☐	☐	☐	☐

VOCABULARY

Use the words in the box to complete the following sentences.

1. When I need a shirt, I go to the _____.
2. To get some money, I go to the _____.
3. To buy a ring, I go to a _____.
4. My washing machine is broken.
   I can get a new one at the _____.
5. My car needs oil. Let's stop at the _____.
6. I need to hang a picture and I don't have any nails. I can buy nails at the _____.
7. My child is sick and the doctor gave me a prescription for medicine for her. I can get the medicine at the
   _____.
8. All my clothes are dirty. I need to go to the _____
   and the _____.

jewelry store
grocery store
bank
childcare center
clothes store
laundromat
gas station
hardware store
computer store
dry cleaner
pharmacy
appliance store
bookstore

READING 7.2

Look at these store advertisements.

MEN'S

3 DAYS ONLY!

semi-annual
CLOTHING
and
DESIGNER
COLLECTIONS
SALE
30% OFF
original prices

**Choose from a terrific selection of
American and European designers.
Everything for your dress and casual
wardrobes. Selections vary by store.**

MARGIN

**GOING
OUT OF
BUSINESS**

30% - 60% OFF

ENTIRE STOCK
OF FURNITURE
CHAIRS
TABLES
SOFAS
ENTERTAINMENT CENTERS
MORE!
CASH ONLY.

**DUCK'S
FURNITURE**

COME TO

LEO'S

WAREHOUSE SALE

SAVE UP TO
70%

**DISHES
GLASSES
UTENSILS
POTS
PANS
... and more!**

TWO DAYS ONLY

Sat June 4th   Sun June 5th
9am to 6pm   10am to 5pm

It's the sale of the year! Our warehouse
is packed with bargains. You won't believe
your eyes, or your wallet!
Bring your family. Bring your friends.

UNDERSTANDING

A. Look at the three ads. Which store should you go to? Check (√) your answer.

	Margin	Duck's	Leo's
1. You want to buy a dining room table.	☐	☐	☐
2. You want to buy a jacket for your father.	☐	☐	☐
3. You need new dinner plates.	☐	☐	☐
4. All of your cups are broken.	☐	☐	☐
5. You have to buy a desk for your son.	☐	☐	☐

B. Look at the three ads. Write *T* if the information is true; write *F* if the information is false.

_____ 1. Margin's sale is once a year.

_____ 2. All the Margin stores have the same clothes on sale.

_____ 3. Duck's Furniture is going out of business.

_____ 4. Everything is on sale at Duck's Furniture.

_____ 5. You can use a credit card at Duck's Furniture.

_____ 6. Leo's Warehouse Sale is for 3 days.

_____ 7. Leo's Warehouse opens at 6 a.m. on Saturday.

_____ 8. Everything is 70% off at Leo's Warehouse sale.

_____ 9. Everything is at least 30% off at Duck's Furniture.

_____ 10. There is a sale of men's and women's clothes at Margin.

C. Look at the ads. Find a word in the ads that means the same as the words below.

1. spoons, knives, forks, for example _____

2. couches _____

3. money _____

4. things on sale for a very good price _____

5. great; excellent _____

THINK ABOUT IT

Why does Duck's Furniture ad say *cash only*?

Leo's Warehouse ad says that you can save up to 70%. Is this a good sale? Why or why not?

BEFORE READING 7.3

Do you ever shop by mail? If so, what kinds of things do you buy by mail? Do you like shopping by mail? Why or why not?

READING 7.3

Look at all the descriptions below.
Match the descriptions with the pictures.

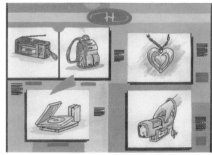

Tutto Pavarotti
"Tutto" is Italian for "all," and this collection is <u>all</u> Pavarotti, the famous opera singer, singing all of his greatest songs from 1968 -1993. 31 songs on 2 cassettes or compact discs.
2 Cassettes...$16   2 Compact Discs...$26 Please add shipping, handling, and tax.

From the Heart
Give this necklace to the woman you love. It's made of sterling silver or gold. Your choice.
Sterling silver...$55   Gold...$175. Please add shipping, handling, and tax.

No batteries! No electricity needed!
With this little radio, you can always listen to music or news. It gets its energy from the sun. If there's no light, there's no problem. For every minute you turn the handle, you get 10 minutes of radio time.
Solar radio... $38 plus shipping, handling, and tax.

Be Safe! Flashlight Alarm
Your keys, an alarm, a flashlight — all in one. Feel safe when you're walking alone at night. With your keys in your hand, you're also holding an alarm and flashlight. Requires 2 AAA batteries (not included).
Flashlight Alarm... $17 plus shipping, handling, and tax.

Holds everything!
Strong and roomy. This beautiful leather backpack comes from Norway. Brown or black leather. Three outside pockets.
Leather Backpack... $89.00 plus shipping, handling, and tax.

AFTER READING 7.3

Look at the items on page 48. Check (√) the correct box or boxes.

	the cassettes	the compact discs	the necklace	the radio	the flashlight alarm	the backpack
1. Which items are less than $25?	☐	☐	☐	☐	☐	☐
2. Which items are more than $50?	☐	☐	☐	☐	☐	☐
3. Which items are for listening enjoyment?	☐	☐	☐	☐	☐	☐
4. Which items can be for both women and men?	☐	☐	☐	☐	☐	☐
5. Which items are useful?	☐	☐	☐	☐	☐	☐
6. Which item needs batteries?	☐	☐	☐	☐	☐	☐
7. Which item would you like best? (Just one!)	☐	☐	☐	☐	☐	☐

LOOKING AT WORDS

1. **Fill in the blanks with information about the pictures.**

a plastic fork   a metal chair   a cotton sweater   gold earrings   a silver necklace

a. This necklace is made of ___*silver*___.   d. This sweater is made of _____.
b. This fork is made of _____.   e. These earrings are made of _____.
c. This chair is made of _____.

2. **Look at the circled words. What nouns do they refer to? Draw an arrow to those nouns.**

a. Do you see that man? (His) daughter is in my class.

b. Give this necklace to someone you love. (It) is made of sterling silver.

c. With this little radio, you can always listen to music. (It) gets its energy from the sun.

d. This beautiful leather backpack comes from Norway. (It) comes in brown or black leather.

CHALLENGE

There are five stores on Park Avenue between First Street and Second Street. The stores include a bakery, a butcher store, a grocery store, a hardware store, and a pharmacy. One person works in each store. Can you figure out where each store is and who works in each store? (Hint: pay attention to the words *Mr., Mrs., Miss,* and *Ms.*)

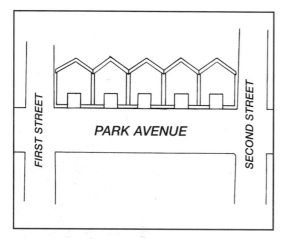

1. The bakery is not next to Mr. Lee's store or the pharmacy.
2. The butcher is a man.
3. Mrs. Moreno's store always smells good when she removes the bread from the oven.
4. The grocery store is on a corner, next to Ms. Ryan's store.
5. Mrs. Mills, the hardware store owner, is good friends with her two neighbors.
6. The pharmacist and Miss Jansen are neighbors but they don't speak to each other.
7. Mr. Lee's store is exactly in the middle of the street.

STORE	WHO WORKS THERE?
bakery	
butcher store	
grocery store	
hardware store	
pharmacy	

Show the location of each store on the map.

QUOTES AND SAYINGS ABOUT SHOPPING	• *The buyer needs a hundred eyes. The seller needs only one.* • *Buyer beware.*

 Which home would you like to live in? Write 1 next to your first choice. Write 2 next to your second choice. Tell your classmates your choices and your reasons.

☐ a house on the beach, 2 hours from the city

☐ a cabin in the mountains, 2 hours from the city

☐ a penthouse apartment in the city with a view

☐ a suburban house and yard, 1 hour from the city center

☐ a mobile home

☐ a house in the city, 1/2 hour from the city center

 Talk with a classmate. Take turns asking and answering these questions.

1. Do you live in an apartment or a house?
2. How many bedrooms are there in your house or apartment?
3. What do you like about your house or apartment?
4. What don't you like about your house or apartment?

READING 8.1

You're invited to
a housewarming party!!!

When? _Sunday, October 15_

Where? _12 Main Place_

Please R.S.V.P. to

Chris or Sandra

Dear Roni,

I hope you are free next Sunday to come to our housewarming party.

Our "new" house is just wonderful! Finally, we have enough room for everyone. There are three bedrooms: one for Chris and me, one for the twins, and one for the baby. The living room is my favorite place because it has a fireplace and a beautiful view of the nearby mountains.

The house isn't perfect. It needs paint and some repairs... but we don't mind.

Yesterday, I met the neighbor down the road. She's a widow and seems very friendly.

I can't wait for you to visit!

Love,
Sandra

Dear Sandra and Chris,

Congratulations on your new home! Of course I can come. I'm looking forward to seeing the house, you two, and the kids.

By the way, what colors are in the kitchen? the bathroom? the living room? Do you need anything special for the house? See you next Sunday!

Love,

Roni

VOCABULARY

housewarming party _n._ a party to celebrate a new house or apartment
R. S. V. P. call or write to say if you can attend or not

UNDERSTANDING

A. Read the invitation and letters. Write _T_ if the sentence is true. Write _F_ if the sentence is false.

_____ 1. The housewarming party is on a Sunday.
_____ 2. Sandra's new house has 3 rooms.
_____ 3. Sandra's new house is in perfect condition.
_____ 4. Sandra likes her bedroom best.
_____ 5. Sandra's neighbor is a friendly man.

B. The answers to questions 6 to 10 are not in the reading word-for-word but you can figure them out if you think about what you read. Again, write _T_ if the sentence is true and write _F_ if the sentence is false.

_____ 6. Chris is the family dog.
_____ 7. Sandra's old house was the same size as this new house.
_____ 8. Sandra likes having a fireplace.
_____ 9. There is a window in the living room.
_____ 10. Roni wants to buy Sandra a gift for her new house.

THINK ABOUT IT

Do the people you know have housewarming parties? What do your friends and family do when someone moves into a new house?

VOCABULARY

Put the words in the box under the best category.

Colors	Rooms	Furniture	Places
red			

red	farm
city	couch
purple	kitchen
country	yellow
living room	bedroom
coffee table	pink
beach	bathroom
dining room	mountain
green	dresser
dining table	bookcase

READING 8.2

Look at the ads for apartment and house rentals in *The International Herald Tribune.*

SAN FRANCISCO. Penthouse apt. City lights/Golden Gate Bridge views. 1 br./1ba. Modern kitchen. A/C. Unfurnished. Non-smoker only. Available immediately. Year lease. $1500/mo. Tel: 415-368-4331

VANCOUVER, CANADA. Oceanfront house. 4 br./3 ba; modern; all new appliances; 2 fireplaces; unfurnished. 3 car garage. 1/2 hour to city ctr. $2000/mo. Tel. 604-293-1533

Barby Park
Executive apartments
• Next to the Shangri La Hotel
• Only 5 minutes from Park

TOKYO. Studio apt. 1/2 hr. from Shinjuku; nr. subway/bus. Heat/air-con. Unfurnished. ¥130,000/mo. Tel: 813-3181-6429

BANGKOK. Attractive 2 br., 2 ba., apt. nr. RCA and hospital; furnished; direct tel, cable TV, pool, parking, security. Available only for July/August. No children. No pets. Bht. 45,000/ mo. Tel:662-318-8224

MEXICO CITY. Quiet neighborhood. 3 br./ 3 ba. house. Big yard. Nr. schools and shopping. Furnished. New carpet and appliances. Garage and security. N$1500 /mo.Tel. 525-669-3014.

VOCABULARY

A/C	*n.*	air conditioning
appliances	*n.*	machines such as washer, dryer, dishwasher, stove, refrigerator
apt.	*n.*	apartment
ba.	*n.*	bathroom
bldg.	*n.*	building
BHT baht		the currency of Thailand
br.	*n.*	bedroom
ctr.	*n.*	center
furnished	*adj.*	with furniture and appliances
incl.	*prep.*	including
lease	*n.*	agreement to rent for a period of time, usually one or two years
mo.		month
N$ pesos	*n.*	the currency of Mexico
nr.	*prep.*	near
unfurnished	*adj.*	without furniture or appliances
¥ yen		the currency of Japan

UNDERSTANDING

A. Look at the floorplans and pictures. Match them to the location of the apartment or house on page 54.

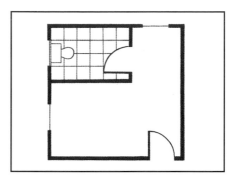

San Francisco

Vancouver

Tokyo

Bangkok

Mexico City

B. Answer the questions about these people's housing needs.

1. The Kim family needs an apartment in Bangkok for five months. Should they look at the advertised apartment? _____ Why or why not?_____

2. The Brown family needs an apartment in San Francisco for two months. Should they look at the advertised apartment? _____ Why or why not? _____

3. Maria Rivas wants to live in the center of Tokyo (very close to the Shinjuku neighborhood). Should she look at the advertised apartment? _____ Why or why not?_____

4. When they move to San Francisco for a year, the Takahashi family doesn't want to bring their furniture and they don't want to buy new furniture. Should they look at the advertised apartment? _____ Why or why not? _____

5. Carlos Espinosa wants a house with two or more bedrooms when he moves to Mexico City. He doesn't care if it is furnished or unfurnished but he wants a quiet place. Should he look at the advertised house? _____ Why or why not? _____

6. Karl Berg wants to rent an apartment in Bangkok for two months. He doesn't plan to bring his dog but he will bring his cat. Should he look at the advertised apartment? _____ Why or why not? _____

BEFORE READING 8.3

Look at the title of the article and the picture. What do you think this article is about? Check (√) your guess.

_____	the color of money around the world
_____	how color affects people's feelings
_____	people of different races
_____	using color to make a house more beautiful

Now read the first paragraph. Was your guess correct? What do you think this article is about?

THINK ABOUT IT

What colors are the walls in your bedroom?
What colors are the walls in your living room?
What colors are the walls in your classroom?

READING 8.3

The Power of Color

1   Are you nervous? Maybe you should sit in a blue room. Are you always cold? Maybe you should sit in a room painted in a "warm color" such as soft orange. Are you often sad? Maybe you should sit in a yellow room. Some researchers believe that color has the power to affect our feelings. They believe that colors affect almost everyone in the same
5   way. They tested this idea in different settings.

One study was in a workplace. The researchers painted heavy boxes white and they painted light boxes black. They wanted to see how color affected the workers' feelings. Which boxes do you think were more difficult to lift? The heavy white ones? No. The black boxes were
10   more difficult. The white boxes were heavier but they looked light. The researchers think that this is because light colors *seem* light.

Another study was at a hospital with brown and green-grey walls. Painters repainted the hospital walls in bright colors--bright orange on the first floor, bright pink on the second floor, bright green on the third floor. What do you think happened? The hospital says the patients changed.
15   They visited each other and talked more. The hospital says the workers also changed and were happier about work.

Another study was in a school. Researchers at the University of Alberta in Edmonton, Canada studied children with behavior problems in their classroom. When the walls were brown and yellow, the children's heart rate went up and they were over-active. When the walls were light and dark blue, the children's heart rate was slower and the children were much calmer.
20   If this is true, people might want to think carefully about the colors around them--not just in houses, but also in offices, in schools, in hospitals, in gyms, in prisons, in museums, and in restaurants!

VOCABULARY

calm	*adj.*	peaceful
gym	*n.*	a place where people exercise
museum	*n.*	a place to see great art
overactive	*adj.*	doing more than usual
patients	*n.*	sick people
prison	*n.*	a place to house and punish criminals (people who break the law)
researcher	*n.*	a person who studies or tests something

AFTER READING 8.3

1. **What is the main idea of this article? Check (√) the correct answer.**
   - ☐ Children are calmer in light blue rooms.
   - ☐ If you are sad, sit in a yellow room.
   - ☐ A heavy box seems light if it is a light color.
   - ☐ Colors affect people's feelings.

2. **This article uses three examples to show how colors affect people's feelings.**
   Those examples show how color affects people's feelings in the_____.
   - ☐ hospital
   - ☐ workplace
   - ☐ restaurant
   - ☐ school

3. **Paragraph 1 is the introduction. It makes the reader interested in the article. It also often tells the main idea of the article. Which paragraph or paragraphs give examples to support the main idea?**
   - ☐ paragraph 2
   - ☐ paragraph 3
   - ☐ paragraph 4

4. **Colors such as red, yellow, and soft orange make people feel _____.**
   - ☐ cold
   - ☐ warm
   - ☐ sad
   - ☐ tired

5. **Blue makes people feel _____.**
   - ☐ warm
   - ☐ calm
   - ☐ nervous
   - ☐ active

6. **A dark colored box feels _____ than a light colored box.**
   - ☐ lighter
   - ☐ heavier
   - ☐ softer
   - ☐ bigger

7. **True or False?**
   _____ In a gym, it would be good to paint the walls light blue.
   _____ In a prison, it would be good to paint the walls light blue.

LOOKING AT WORDS

A. **Some words have more than one meaning. The word *light* has more than one meaning. Here is a dictionary definition for the adjective *light*.**

light *adj. 1.* not dark in color: *light blue* *2.* not heavy: *This box is light. The little boy can lift it.* *3.* easy to see in: *This room is light because there are many windows.*

Write the number of the definition that matches the word *light* in each sentence.

   __1__ He's wearing a light brown shirt.
   _____ In the morning, the sun makes this room very light.
   _____ She has light green eyes.
   _____ This letter is light. You only need one stamp.
   _____ I can move the table by myself. It's light.

B. **The words *researcher, painter,* and *worker* all end in *-er*. What does the *-er* ending mean in these words? _____**

C. **At the beginning of a word, *re-* sometimes means "again." The word *repaint* means "to paint again." Check (√) the words where *re-* means "again."**

   _____ rewrite   _____ read   _____ recipe
   _____ retest   _____ register   _____ retell
   _____ retired   _____ redo   _____ remarry

CHALLENGE

The words in this crossword puzzle are in Unit 8. Can you complete the crossword puzzle?

Across Clues

1. When it's cold, I like to sit near the _____ in the living room.
3. I want to move this sofa but I can't do it. It's too _____.
5. The_____ is the top apartment in an apartment building.
6. I painted the walls_____blue, not dark blue.
7. Red and white together makes the color _____.
8. People cook in the_____.
10. Apt.

Down Clues

1. He lives on the 15th _____ in that apartment building.
2. What _____ are the walls in your living room--white or blue?
3. Very sick people go to the _____.
4. _____ is a very "warm" color.
5. Someone who paints is a _____.
9. _____ is where the heart is. (See the title of this chapter.)

| QUOTES AND SAYINGS ABOUT HOMES | • *There's no place like home.*

• *Home is where you hang your hat.* |

Look at these pictures. What times of day do they show? Write the time of day under each picture. Use each of the words in the box only once.

dusk	dawn	evening
night	morning	afternoon

_____ _____ _____

_____ _____ _____

Draw a chart showing your average day (1 hour = approximately 4% of the day). Show it to a classmate.

Example

8 hours sleeping

2 hours eating

2 hours cooking/cleaning

2 hours studying

8 hours working

1 hour washing/dressing/grooming

1 hour watching TV

Talk with a classmate. Take turns asking and answering these questions.

1. What time do you get up?
2. What time do you go to bed?
3. What time do you eat lunch?
4. How many hours per week do you study?
5. How many hours per week do you work?
6. How many hours per night do you sleep?

READING 9.1

What time of day do you like best?

Anna Cruz

"I have five children. The house is always busy when they're awake. That's why I try to get up before everyone else. I get up at dawn. The house is quiet. I drink a cup of coffee and read the newspaper. I love that time because it's mine and I can think without interruptions."

Kyung Mi Moon

"I'm a night person. I love the night. I feel sleepy all day and then at night--I wake up! I like to go out dancing or see movies or talk to friends. I never go to sleep before 2 a.m."

Sandra Wu

"I'm a morning person. As soon as a little light comes through the window, I wake up. I never stay in bed. I love to start the day. I try to do important work in the morning because I know that I think best at that time. By 1:00, I begin to slow down!"

Jamal Shirazi

"I like the time around dusk. I try to watch the sunset every day. It gives me a feeling that the day is complete. It's a time for me to think about the day, think about people, think about life."

Jane Reed

"I love tea time. I have tea every afternoon--late afternoon. It's a time to stop the day's activity for an hour, and talk with friends and family. Sometimes, people visit my home then. Sometimes, I go to a friend's house for tea."

Kimio Takano

"I love it when I stop working! If it's 6:00, that's my favorite time. If it's 7:00, that's my favorite time. If it's 10:00, that's my favorite time!"

UNDERSTANDING

A. Look at these illustrations. Match the correct person with the drawing.

Anna Cruz

Kyung Mi Moon

Sandra Wu

Jamal Shirazi

Jane Reed

Kimio Takano

B. Check (√) the correct box or boxes.

	Anna	Kyung Mi	Sandra	Jamal	Jane	Kimio
1. These two people are morning people.	√		√			
2. These people think best in the morning.						
3. This person always goes to bed late.						
4. The favorite time of these people is with friends and/or family.						
5. This person uses her favorite time to work.						
6. This person uses his favorite time to think about life.						

READING 9.2a

At the Honolulu airport, there are signs for "Arrivals" and "Departures". (Note that at airports, the 24 hour clock is used; that is, 1:00 p.m. is the same as 13:00.)

ARRIVALS					
Flight #	**Airline**	**Coming From**	**Arrival Time**	**Gate**	
801	PK Air	Los Angeles	15:00	2	**On time**
1325	KLN Air	Tokyo	15:45	1	**15 minute delay**
277	TAW Air	Sydney	16:00	3	**On time**
222	Transair	Seoul	16:30	2	**On time**
DEPARTURES					
Flight #	**Airline**	**Destination**	**Departure Time**	**Gate**	
19	Volt Air	New York	11:00	1	**Delayed until 14:30**
1724	Transair	Vancouver	15:20	4	**Boarding now**
802	PK Air	Hong Kong	16:00	2	
1326	KLN Air	San Francisco	17:00	1	
223	Transair	Vancouver	17:30	2	

SCANNING

How many questions can you answer in two minutes? Write *T* if the sentence is true; write *F* if the sentence is false.

_____ 1. Flight 1326 goes to San Francisco at 5:00 p.m.
_____ 2. Flight 801 is on time.
_____ 3. Transair Airlines flies to Vancouver.
_____ 4. Flight 1325 is coming into gate 3.
_____ 5. A flight to Vancouver is boarding now.
_____ 6. Flight 1325 is on time.
_____ 7. Only one flight today goes to Vancouver.
_____ 8. Flight 802 leaves at 4:00 a.m.
_____ 9. Flight 19 is delayed more than 3 hours.
_____ 10. The airline that flies to Hong Kong is PK Air.
_____ 11. Volt Air flies to New York.
_____ 12. PK Air leaves the airport at 6 p.m.
_____ 13. You should meet your friend from Sydney at Gate 3 at 4:00 p.m.
_____ 14. Flight 801 from Los Angeles arrives at 3 p.m.
_____ 15. The flight from Sydney arrives when the flight to Hong Kong departs.

READING 9.2b

Look at these messages. Match each message with (1) the picture of the meeting place and (2) the meeting time.

JIM,

MEET ME AT THE TAW COUNTER AT 4:00 I'M LOOKING FORWARD TO SEEING YOU!

JOE

Carla,

The bus leaves the airport every hour on the hour. Take the six o'clock bus. I'll wait for you at the bus stop on 4th Street and Main Street. The trip takes almost an hour. See you soon.

Maria

Akemi,

Wait for me near the baggage claim area. I have to be a little late but don't worry. I'll be there around 5:00. The Takanos are expecting us for dinner at 7:00. We can't wait to see you!

Mayumi

BEFORE READING 9.3

Look at the title and the pictures. What do you think this reading will be about? Check (√) one guess.

_____	different kinds of clocks
_____	how to take care of clocks
_____	how to manage time
_____	a housewife's average day

Talk with a classmate. Take turns asking and answering these questions.

Do you think you use your time well? Why or why not?

READING 9.3

The Clock Is Ticking

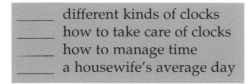

There are 24 hours in a day--no more, no less. Yet we often hear people say, "There aren't enough hours in a day." People are always trying to do too much--working, reading, exercising, playing sports, watching TV, visiting friends, taking care of children, shopping, cooking, cleaning--and of course, sleeping! Sometimes, it's impossible to do everything. That's when people need to learn about "time management," the skill of using time well.

Here are some "tips" for time management:

• <u>Set priorities.</u> You must decide what is most important and what is less important. One way to do this is to write down all the things you want to do. Then, put an "A" next to things that are most important and urgent. Put a "B" next to things that are less important and less urgent. Put a "C" next to things that are even less important and even less urgent. The letter "A" marks your first priorities.

• <u>Make a daily "to do" list.</u> Set priorities on your list. Write down how much time you need to do each item.

• <u>Be honest about the time you have and the time you need to do things.</u> If there isn't enough time, you must reduce your list.

• <u>Schedule "downtime."</u> No one can run 24 hours per day. Everyone needs time with friends and family, time to relax.

You can't stop time but you can use it well!

```
        TO DO

A   Doctor's appointment
      1 hour

B   Call John

C   Shop

B   Pick up dry cleaning

A   Do homework
      2 hours
```

VOCABULARY

daily	_adj._	done every day
honest	_adj._	truthful
urgent	_adj._	needing care and attention right away

AFTER READING 9.3

1. Look at your guess on page 64. Were you correct?
2. Another good title for this article could be
   _____ How To Use Your Time Well   _____ How To Stop Time
   _____ How To Set Priorities   _____ How To Relax
3. Look at the "To Do" list on page 64. What has the lowest priority on the list? _____
4. How many "tips" for time management does the article give?
   _____

LOOKING AT WORDS

Look at the context of each word and try to guess the correct meaning. Check (√) your guess.

1. In paragraph 1, *it's impossible to do everything* means
   ☐ a. you can do everything.   ☐ b. you can't do everything.

2. In paragraph 1, *time management* is
   ☐ a. the skill of doing too much.   ☐ b. the skill of using time well.   ☐ c. the skill of relaxing.

3. A *tip* is
   ☐ a. advice; good ideas.   ☐ b. bad ideas; bad news.

4. Look at the first tip. *Set priorities* means
   ☐ a. make a list.   ☐ b. decide what is most important, less important, and even less important.

5. Look at the third tip. *If there isn't enough time, you must reduce your list.*
   What must you do if there isn't enough time?
   ☐ a. Make your list longer.   ☐ b. Make your list shorter.   ☐ c. Throw away your list.

6. Look at the fourth tip. *Downtime* is
   ☐ a. busy time.   ☐ b. unimportant time.   ☐ c. time to relax.

TRY IT

Make a "To Do" list for tomorrow. Set priorities. Think about how much time you have and how much time you need.

Work with a classmate. One person is Student A. One person is Student B. Student B reads the fable on this page, "The Goose and the Golden Egg." Student A reads the fable on page 67, "The Boy and the Nuts." Don't look at your classmate's fable! When you both finish reading, do the exercise on the bottom of this page.

The Goose and the Golden Egg

1　There was once a wonderful goose. Everyday, the goose produced a golden egg. Its owners, a husband and wife, were very lucky to have this goose.

However, the owners of the goose were a little greedy. They loved the golden eggs but they wanted more than one golden egg a day. They wanted
5　to get rich faster.

The man looked at his wife and said, "If this goose can produce a golden egg everyday, it must have a lot of gold inside. Why should we wait? One a day. That's too slow. If we cut the goose open, I'm sure there is a lot of gold inside. Then we can be rich right away. What do you think?"

10　The woman agreed with her husband. "Yes. One golden egg a day is nice, but it's very slow. If we open the goose and take all the gold inside, we can use it all now. Let's do it."

The man grabbed knife and cut the goose open. Of course, the goose died.

When the man and woman looked inside the goose, they hoped to find lots
15　of gold but they were surprised. "There's no gold in here. It looks like any other goose," cried the wife.

"Now, what do we have? cried the man. "No riches right away. No golden egg everyday. Just a dead goose.

Listen to your classmate read "The Boy and the Nuts" to you. When he or she finishes telling you the story, number the pictures (1 to 5) in the correct order of the story.

TALK ABOUT IT

What is the message of "The Boy and the Nuts?" What is the message of "The Goose and the Golden Egg?"

People wear jeans all over the world. However, people have different ideas about where jeans are OK. For example, some people think they can wear jeans everywhere: to school, to work, to parties, to the theater. Other people say jeans are OK for sports but not for other activities. What do you think? Check (√) the places where you think it is OK to wear jeans. Tell your classmates why.

at a movie theater

at the office

at a baseball game

at a disco

at university

at a fancy restaurant

at a supermarket

at a church or temple

Play a game with your classmates. One student says, "I am thinking of a classmate. He (or she) is wearing _____." The other students have to guess who it is.

T-shirt

blouse

skirt

dress

pants

jacket

tie

READING 11.1

Dear Roni,

Good news. I get three weeks vacation this year and I'm planning a trip to Southern California in August. Peter can't go with me but I plan to take Elena and Emma. (Wait until you see them! They are so big and they are 5 years old already!) They know that Disneyland is in Southern California. They can't stop talking about it. A picture of Mickey Mouse is on the wall of their room!

Can you recommend a good and reasonably priced hotel in your area? We're going to rent a car so I'll need parking, too.

Also, I'm not sure how to pack. What clothes should I bring? What's the weather like?

Is there anything I can bring you from Canada? Maple syrup?

Please write and let me know.

Love,
Catherine

Dear Catherine,

I'm so excited that you and the girls are coming. Dont even think of staying in a hotel. I have room in my house and I would love to see you. (I think you're right to rent a car. I may need to work, and public transportation is not good in Southern California.)

As for clothes, remember that Southern Californians are very informal. August is very warm and dry so we often wear shorts and a T-shirt or a short-sleeved shirt. The night can be cool so bring a light jacket, pants and jeans. Bring one or two nice outfits for when we go to a nice restaurant or to the theater. And of course, bring a bathing suit. Dont worry about bringing an umbrella or raincoat. It never rains here in August.

Thank you for asking if I want anything from Canada. No thanks! I just want to see you!

Love,
Roni

VOCABULARY

to have room	*v.*	to have empty space for people or things
to pack	*v.*	to put your belongings in a suitcase or bag
public transportation	*n.*	ways to travel that are for everyone, such as bus or train
reasonably priced	*adj.*	not too expensive (but not cheap)

UNDERSTANDING

A. Check (√) the things that Catherine should pack for Southern California in August.

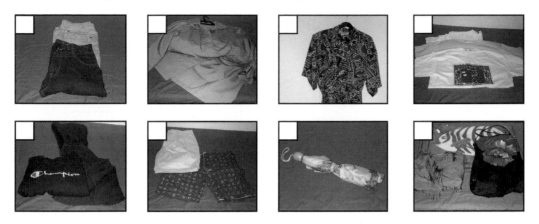

B. Write *T* if the sentence is true. Write *F* if the sentence is false. Write *?* if there isn't enough information in Catherine's and Roni's letters.

_____ 1. Peter is Catherine's husband.
_____ 2. Elena and Emma are twins.
_____ 3. Elena and Emma want to go to Disneyland.
_____ 4. Catherine wants to stay in the best hotel.
_____ 5. Catherine doesn't know about the weather in Southern California in August.
_____ 6. Roni wants Catherine and the girls to stay at her house.
_____ 7. Roni recommends renting a car because the buses and trains in Southern California are not very good.
_____ 8. Roni wants Catherine to bring an umbrella to California.

VOCABULARY

Mary   David   Junko   Joe   Nora

Look at the pictures and descriptions. There is one mistake in each description. Find the mistake and correct it.

1. Mary is wearing a ~~long~~ *short*-sleeved blouse and skirt. She isn't wearing a jacket. She's wearing stockings and high-heel shoes. She's wearing a small hat.
2. David is wearing a suit and tie. He is carrying a coat and an umbrella. He is wearing shoes and socks.
3. Junko is dressed for the office. She is wearing a women's suit and a dark blouse. She is wearing stockings and low-heeled shoes. She's carrying a handbag.
4. Joe is going to a soccer game. He is wearing a cap, a T-shirt, pants and socks. He is also wearing sunglasses.
5. Nora is wearing a bathing suit and sandals. Her sunglasses are on her head. She is carrying a towel and a radio.

READING 11.2

Look at the clothes and their labels.

100% Cotton
Made in
Sri Lanka.

Machine Wash
Cold with
Similar Colors.
Tumble Dry Low.
Steam Iron.

100% Silk
Made in China.

Dry-Clean or
Machine Wash
Warm.Tumble
Dry Low.
Cool Iron.

100% Silk
Made in U.S.A.

Dry-Clean Only.

100% Polyester
Made in France.

Machine Wash
Warm. Color May
Transfer When New.
Wash Once Before
Wearing.

100% Wool
Made in
England.

Dry-Clean
Only.

100% Cotton
Made in
El Salvador.

Hand Wash
in Cold Water.
Hang to Dry.
Do not Iron.

65% Polyester
35% Cotton.
Made in Taiwan.

Machine Wash
Cold.
Tumble Dry Low.
Wash with
Dark Colors Only.

VOCABULARY

similar *adj.* almost the same
reverse *n.* the other side

Tumble Dry

Steam Iron

Hang

UNDERSTANDING

Check (√) the correct box or boxes.

	the T-shirt	the long-sleeved shirt	the tie	the pants	the jacket	the dress	the sweater
1. Which items are made of 100% natural materials?							
2. Which items are made in Asia?							
3. Which items must you dry-clean only?							
4. Which item can you dry-clean and machine wash?							
5. Which item should you wash by hand?							
6. Which items should you iron?							
7. Which items should you only wash with similar colors?							
8. Which items should you wash in cold water?							

TALK ABOUT IT

Do you go to a laundromat? Do you have a washer in your house? Do you dry-clean any clothes? What kind? Do you handwash any clothes? What kind? Do you iron any clothes? What kind?

BEFORE READING 11.3

A. **Look at the title and the picture. What do you think the article is about? Check (√) your answer.**

> _____ the man who created blue jeans
> _____ men who wear blue jeans
> _____ men's clothes before blue jeans
> _____ jeans for men and women

B. **Do you wear jeans? Are jeans popular in your country? If so, who wears them—young people, older people, all people?**

READING 11.3

The Man Behind Blue Jeans

1　　Levi Strauss was born in 1829 in Bavaria, Germany. He was the fifth of six children. His father sold dry goods from door to door. (Dry goods include 5 many different things: fabric, thread, scissors, combs, buttons, yarn, etc.)

　　In 1845, his father died. All six children decided to go to the 10 United States. Two of Strauss' brothers started a dry goods company in New York City. Strauss' sister Fanny and her husband started a similar 15 business in San Francisco. Strauss decided to go to the southeastern part of the United States. For eight years, he walked the country roads selling dry goods from door to door—just 20 like his father in Bavaria.

　　In 1853, Strauss decided to move to San Francisco. (At that time, thousands of people traveled to California to look for gold.) On the way to California, Strauss sold almost all of his dry goods. He had only one thing left—some 25 canvas (a very heavy fabric).

　　In California, Strauss tried to sell the canvas to the gold miners. He said they could make tents from the canvas. But they 30 weren't interested in canvas for tents. Strauss didn't know what to do with the canvas. Then, he had an idea. Strauss could see that the miners needed new 35 pants. There were holes in their pants because the fabric wasn't strong. He decided to make the canvas into pants. The miners loved his pants. They called 40 them "Levi's." Later, Strauss stopped using canvas and used a different fabric. It was a heavy cotton fabric—the same kind people wear today.

　　Levi Strauss died in 1902. He never married and left his money to his nephews. He left the world 45 much more—the jeans that so many people wear.

VOCABULARY

scissors
comb
button
thread
yarn

dry goods　　　　hole　　　　miner

tent

AFTER READING 11.3

A. Look at your guess on page 74. Were you correct?

B. Look at the pictures below. Number them from 1-7 showing the events in Strauss' life.

San Francisco

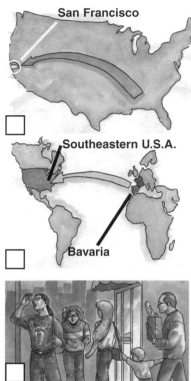
Southeastern U.S.A.

Bavaria

1

LOOKING AT WORDS

A. Many words in the reading are in the past tense. Most past tense words have an-*ed* ending but some are irregular. Look through the article and find the irregular past tense words.
   1. The past tense of sell is _____.
   2. The past tense of have is _____.
   3. The past tense of leave is _____.

B. Levi Strauss was the fifth of six children. Look at the picture of the Strauss family. Which boy is probably Levi? Circle him in the picture.

The Strauss Family

The Soto Family

Maria Soto is the second of four children. Look at the picture of the Soto family. Which one is probably Maria? Circle her in the picture.

Where are you in your family?

"I am the _____ of_____ children" or "I am an only child."

CHALLENGE

Can you find these 25 pieces of clothing and colors in the puzzle? You may find the words vertically(↕), horizontally(↔), or diagonally(⤢).

Colors

black	pink
blue	purple
brown	red
green	white
orange	yellow

Clothes

bathrobe	shirt
blouse	shorts
dress	skirt
hat	socks
jacket	stockings
jeans	suit
pants	sweater
	tie

A	B	B	L	U	E	D	R	O	S	S	Y	G
C	D	S	L	B	L	O	U	S	E	E	E	R
W	F	H	G	A	R	H	P	U	R	P	L	E
H	J	O	I	T	C	O	J	I	K	A	L	E
I	A	R	L	H	S	K	W	T	M	N	O	N
T	C	T	N	R	O	P	O	N	P	T	W	S
E	K	S	T	O	C	K	I	N	G	S	I	J
R	E	D	T	B	K	U	W	N	A	K	B	E
C	T	S	W	E	A	T	E	R	K	I	D	A
E	N	O	P	O	R	A	N	G	E	R	E	N
O	D	R	E	S	S	S	H	I	R	T	E	S

QUOTES AND SAYINGS ABOUT CLOTHING	• *A stitch in time saves nine.* • *The shoemaker's children always go barefoot.*

How do you stay healthy? Check (√) the things you do to stay healthy. Tell your classmates your answers.

☐ I play sports.

☐ I eat healthy foods.

☐ I meditate.

☐ I take vitamins.

☐ I walk a lot.

☐ I ride a bicycle.

☐ I work out in a gym.

☐ I jog.

☐ I do aerobics.

☐ I swim.

Talk to a classmate. Take turns asking and answering these questions.

On a scale from 1-4, how healthy are you? (1 is very unhealthy, 2 is a little unhealthy, 3 is pretty healthy, 4 is very healthy.)

1. What healthy foods do you eat?
2. Do you take vitamins?
3. Do you go to a gym?
4. What exercise do you get?

READING 12.2

Sometimes, people feel sick and need to take medicine. Look at these medicines and their labels.

1. **For headaches**

Dosage:

> **Adults and Children 12 Years of Age and Over:**
> 1 to 2 tablets every four hours
> **Children 6 to 12 Years of Age:** 1/2 to 1 tablet
> every six hours
> **Children Under 6 Years of Age:** Consult a doctor.

Directions: Take tablets after meals.

HED·EX

2. **For coughs**

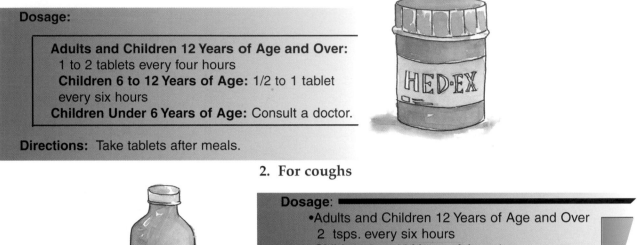

SUPPRESINN

Dosage:
• Adults and Children 12 Years of Age and Over
  2 tsps. every six hours
• Children 6 to 12 Years of Age: 1 tsp. every
  six hours
• Children 2 to 6 Years of Age: 1/2 tsp. every
  six hours
Do not give to children under 2 years of age.

Directions: Drink one glass of water after taking
medicine.

3. **For aches and pains**

For Adults and Children 6 Years of Age and Over.
Directions:
> Apply to the painful area 3 or 4 times daily.
> Do not apply near eyes or nose.

For external use only

RELIEF

VOCABULARY

aches and pains *n.*	something hurts
to apply *v.*	to put on
to consult *v.*	to talk to for advice
dosage *n.*	the amount to take
external *adj.*	outside
meals *n.*	breakfast, lunch, or dinner
ointment *n.*	a medicine that you rub on skin

UNDERSTANDING

A. Look at the medicines and their labels on page 80. Check (√) the correct answers.

1. Megumi's son is 4 years old. He has a terrible headache. Megumi should
    _____ a. give him medicine 1
    _____ b. give him medicine 2
    _____ c. give him medicine 3
    _____ d. not give him medicine 1, 2, or 3. Maybe she should consult a doctor.

2. Megumi has a headache. She should
    _____ a. take medicine 1
    _____ b. take medicine 2
    _____ c. take medicine 3

3. What dosage should Megumi take for her headache?
    _____ a. 1 to 2 tablets every four hours
    _____ b. 2 tsp. every six hours
    _____ c. 1/2 to 1 tablet every six hours
    _____ d. 1 tsp. every six hours

4. Megumi's daughter is 3 years old. She has a bad cough. Megumi wants to give her some "Suppresinn" cough medicine. How much should she give her?
    _____ a. 2 tsp. every six hours
    _____ b. 1 tsp. every six hours
    _____ c. 1/2 tsp. every six hours

B. True or False? Write _T_ if the statement is true; write _F_ if the statement is false.

_____ 1. You should eat after you take the headache tablets.
_____ 2. You should drink a glass of water after you take the cough medicine.
_____ 3. You should eat the "aches and pains" ointment.
_____ 4. You should put the "aches and pains" ointment near your eyes and nose.
_____ 5. Children six years age and over can use the "aches and pains" ointment.

TALK ABOUT IT

What do you do when you have a cough?
What do you do when you have a backache?
What do you do when you have a stomachache?
What do you do when you have a headache?

BEFORE READING 12.3

Look at the title and the picture. What do you think this article is about? Check (√) one guess.

_____ a story of one person's illness
_____ ways to prevent and treat headaches
_____ why people get headaches

READING 12.3

My Aching Head!

1 Everyone gets headaches. Some people get them very often. Other people are lucky--they only get them once in a while.

5 There are some ways to prevent headaches. They don't work 100% of the time but they can reduce the number of headaches you get.

- Eat regular meals. Don't skip
10 meals.
- Get enough sleep.
- Try to avoid stress.
- Get fresh air and exercise.
- Avoid drinking a lot of coffee or alcohol.

15 What should you do when you get a headache? How can you treat it? There are many different ways. (If you ask ten people what they do when they get a headache, you might hear ten different answers!) Here are some suggestions:

20 • Relax in a warm bath.
- Massage in a circular motion behind your ear and across the back of your neck.
- Massage your scalp (as if you are washing your hair). Gently pull the hair all around your 25 head.
- While sitting, breathe in and bend your head back gently, looking up at the ceiling. Don't bend too far back. Breathe out and 30 bring your head down so that your chin rests on your chest. Repeat two times.
- Breathe out and turn your head to look over your right 35 shoulder. Don't bend your chin to your shoulder. Keep your chin level. Breathe as you turn your head back, looking straight ahead. Do the same thing over your left shoulder. Repeat two times on each side. 40
- Take medicine, such as aspirin.

Why don't you try one of these the next time you get a headache? See what works for you.

VOCABULARY

to avoid something	_v._	to not go near or not do something
once in a while		not all the time; sometimes
to prevent	_v._	to stop something from happening
to reduce	_v._	to lower the number
to skip a meal	_v._	to not eat breakfast, lunch or dinner

AFTER READING 12.3

1. Look at your guess on page 82. Were you correct?

2. How many suggestions does the article give for preventing headaches?
   _____

3. How many suggestions does the article give for treating headaches?
   _____

4. Which of the following is a way to avoid headaches? Check (√) one.

   ☐ massage your neck   ☐ take an aspirin
   ☐ get enough sleep   ☐ relax in a warm bath

5. Watch your teacher. Which headache treatment is she or he doing?

   ☐ "Massage in a circular motion behind your ears."
   ☐ "Massage in a circular motion across the back of your neck."
   ☐ "Massage your scalp (as if you are washing your hair). Gently pull the hair all around your head."
   ☐ "While sitting, breathe in and bend your head back gently, looking up at the ceiling. Breathe out and bring your head down so that your chin rests on your chest."
   ☐ "Breathe out and turn your head to look over your right shoulder. Keep your chin level. Breathe in as you turn your head back, looking straight ahead."

6. Watch your teacher a second time. Which headache treatment is she or he doing now?

   ☐ "Massage in a circular motion behind your ears."
   ☐ "Massage in a circular motion across the back of your neck."
   ☐ "Massage your scalp (as if you are washing your hair). Gently pull the hair all around your head."
   ☐ "While sitting, breathe in and bend your head back gently, looking up at the ceiling. Breathe out and bring your head down so that your chin rests on your chest."
   ☐ "Breathe out and turn your head to look over your right shoulder. Keep your chin level. Breathe in as you turn your head back, looking straight ahead."

LOOKING AT LANGUAGE

The words *such as, for example,* and *for instance,* tell you that examples will follow. Complete the sentences with some examples.

1. She loves sports such as _____ and _____ .
2. He hates green vegetables, for example, _____ and _____.
3. I want to visit some countries in Asia, for instance, _____ and _____.

CHALLENGE

All of the words in this crossword puzzle are in Unit 12. Can you complete the crossword puzzle?

Across

1. Bring your head down so your _____ _____ rests on your chest.
3. The _____ of that medicine for children is one tablet every four hours.
4. Tennis, basketball, and soccer are _____.
5. Teaspoon.
7. Some people go to a _____ to get exercise.
10. The opposite of sit.
11. He has a pain in his head. He has a head _____.
12. He can't _____ because there is no air.

Down

2. The opposite of *sick* is _____.
6. You play this sport with a black and white round ball. Pele was a famous player of this sport.
8. Breakfast is often the first _____ of the day.
9. Some people like to _____ by watching TV or reading a book.
10. I like warm colors _____ as red, yellow, and orange.

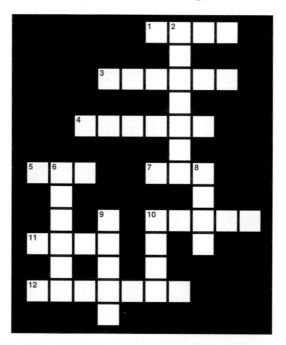

QUOTES AND SAYINGS ABOUT HEALTH	• *Early to bed and early to rise makes a man healthy, wealthy, and wise.* • *An apple a day keeps the doctor away.*

Can you match these people with their baby pictures?
Work with a classmate.

Bring baby or childhood pictures to class and post them on the board.
Talk about yourself as a child or baby and see if your classmates can find your picture.

Example:

In my picture, I am wearing a blue and white dress and white shoes. I am sitting down. I have short brown hair and big blue eyes. I look happy.

READING 13.1

Dear Catherine,

I'm so sorry I can't pick you up at the airport but luckily, my friend Steve can. (He works at night, so he is free in the morning.)

I just want to make sure about the information. Your plane arrives at 11 a.m. on June 25th and you're flying on KLN Air #1327. Is that right?

I told Steve to look for a woman with two young girls but he wanted more information. Do you look the same? What about your daughters?

You shouldn't have a problem finding Steve at the airport. He's very tall and thin. He has curly brown hair, a moustache, and a beard.

I can't wait to see you!

Love,

Roni

Dear Roni,

Please thank your friend, Steve. It's very nice of him to pick us up at the airport.

I do look different from the last time we saw each other. My hair is long and wavy now... and I have a lot more gray hair! I don't wear glasses anymore. (I wear contact lenses.) Of course I'm still short and a little overweight! That never changes!

Elena and Emma are five years old. They both look like Peter, not me. They have his dark, brown eyes and straight black hair. Elena's hair is very long - down to her waist! Emma's hair is short.

Well - no more writing for now! See you in a few days!

Love,

Catherine

UNDERSTANDING

A. There are lots of people at the airport. Can you find Catherine, Emma, Elena, and Steve? Write the numbers.

_____Catherine

_____Emma

_____Elena

_____Steve

B. True or False? Write *T* if the statement is true. Write *F* if the statement is false.

_____ 1. Roni can't pick up Catherine and the girls at the airport.
_____ 2. Peter looks like Catherine.
_____ 3. Elena and Emma look exactly the same.
_____ 4. Catherine is arriving in a few days.
_____ 5. Catherine always looks the same.

VOCABULARY

There is a mistake in each description. Find the mistake and correct it.

1. Tamara has wavy, black, shoulder-length hair. She is very heavy. She is wearing earrings.

2. In Sook has straight black hair. It goes down to her waist. She wears glasses.

3. Mario has curly, black hair. He has a moustache. He is wearing one earring.

4. Leo has a beard and moustache. He is bald. He wears glasses.

READING 13.2

Look at the newspaper advertisements. What are these people looking for?

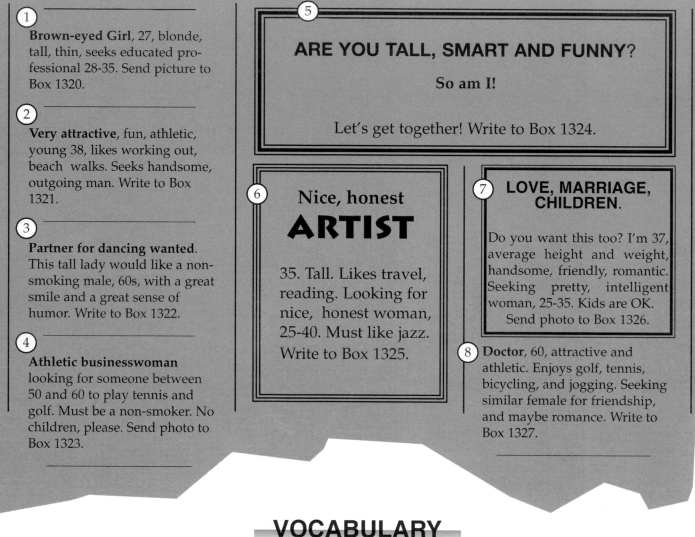

① Brown-eyed Girl, 27, blonde, tall, thin, seeks educated professional 28-35. Send picture to Box 1320.

② Very attractive, fun, athletic, young 38, likes working out, beach walks. Seeks handsome, outgoing man. Write to Box 1321.

③ Partner for dancing wanted. This tall lady would like a non-smoking male, 60s, with a great smile and a great sense of humor. Write to Box 1322.

④ Athletic businesswoman looking for someone between 50 and 60 to play tennis and golf. Must be a non-smoker. No children, please. Send photo to Box 1323.

⑤ ARE YOU TALL, SMART AND FUNNY?

So am I!

Let's get together! Write to Box 1324.

⑥ Nice, honest

ARTIST

35. Tall. Likes travel, reading. Looking for nice, honest woman, 25-40. Must like jazz. Write to Box 1325.

⑦ LOVE, MARRIAGE, CHILDREN.

Do you want this too? I'm 37, average height and weight, handsome, friendly, romantic. Seeking pretty, intelligent woman, 25-35. Kids are OK. Send photo to Box 1326.

⑧ Doctor, 60, attractive and athletic. Enjoys golf, tennis, bicycling, and jogging. Seeking similar female for friendship, and maybe romance. Write to Box 1327.

VOCABULARY

outgoing	*adj.*	friendly person who likes meeting people
professional	*adj.*	a person with a job that requires advanced education
romantic	*adj.*	doing things to make your partner feel special and loved
working out	*v.*	taking physical exercise

UNDERSTANDING

Check (√) the correct box or boxes.

	①	②	③	④	⑤	⑥	⑦	⑧
a. Who wants someone funny?								
b. Who likes sports?								
c. Who doesn't want a smoker?								
d. Who wants to see a photograph?								
e. Who is looking for a professional?								
f. Who is a professional?								

TALK ABOUT IT

Do people advertise for friends or dates or marriage partners in your country? If so, are the ads similar to the ones on page 88?

THINK ABOUT IT

There are 8 ads on page 88. Are any of those people a good match for each other? Which ones?

TRY IT

What would you say about yourself in an ad? What kind of person would you look for? Write an ad.

BEFORE READING 13.3

A. Look at the title and the pictures. What do you think this article will be about? Check (√) one answer.

_____ twins who got lost in a department store
_____ twins who fight a lot with each other
_____ twins who were separated but came together again
_____ how to tell the difference between twins

B. Ask your classmates:

Are you a twin? If so, do you look like your twin? Do you act like your twin? Do you know any twins? If so, do they look alike? Do they act alike?

READING 13.3

When "Lost" Twins Find Each Other

1   One day in 1982, Barbara Parker, 61, had a big surprise! Her neighbor walked into her house and said, "I've got your twin sister Ann sitting in my living
5   room."

    "What twin sister?" Barbara was surprised because she didn't know about her twin sister. When Barbara was born, the Parkers adopted her.
10   Her new parents raised her as an only child.

    When the neighbor saw Barbara and Ann together, she couldn't believe her eyes. She said, "Look, you move your hands the same way! You
15   stand the same! You laugh the same!" When the neighbor asked what they wanted to drink, they both said, "Tea, lukewarm."

During the following weeks and months, the two women learned more about each other. Both married young and   20   had two children. Both were hairdressers. Both sew well and made many of their children's clothes. Both are good dancers and singers. Both, as teenagers,   25   were athletic and loved softball. (Ann chipped a tooth playing softball. Barbara chipped the same tooth years later.) The two women even had the same bedspread!   30

    Their meeting changed their lives. "Meeting Barbara helped me find out who I am," says Ann. Barbara probably feels the same way about Ann!

VOCABULARY

to adopt	_v._	to take someone else's child and raise him or her as your own child
bedspread	_n._	a covering for a bed
to chip	_v._	to break a small piece off
lukewarm	_adj._	not very hot

A. Look at your guess on page 90. Were you correct?

B. Don't look back at the story. How much can you remember about the twins? Write four more similarities below.

1. Both ___*Barbara and Ann laugh the same*___.

2. Both _____.

3. Both _____.

4. Both _____.

5. Both _____.

LOOKING AT WORDS

A. Many words in the reading are in the past tense. Most past tense words have an *ed* end but some words are irregular. Look through the article and find the irregular past tense words.

The past tense of *have* is _____.
The past tense of *say* is _____.
The past tense of *make* is _____.
The past tense of *be* is _____ or _____.

B. Look at the circled word. What does it refer to? Draw an arrow to the word or words.

1. My friend lives in London. Her husband works there.
2. Barbara was surprised because she didn't know about her twin sister.
3. When the neighbor saw Barbara and Ann together, she couldn't believe her eyes.
4. When the neighbor saw Barbara and Ann together, she couldn't believe her eyes. When the neighbor asked what they wanted to drink, they both said, "Tea, lukewarm."
5. Barbara and Ann both sew well and made many of their children's clothes.

CHALLENGE

Three men (Lee, Joe, and Ken) and three women (Kim, Celia, and Maria) are going on blind dates. One couple is going to the movies. One is going out dancing. One couple is going to a basketball game. Can you figure out the couples' names and where they are going?

1. Lee is short and only dates short women.
2. Celia and Maria hate sports and never watch or play them.
3. Ken has a moustache and smokes a pipe.
4. Celia only dates non-smokers.
5. Lee is going to take his date to the movies.
6. Celia is a very tall woman.
7. Maria has shoulder-length black, wavy hair.

_____ and _____ are going dancing.

_____ and _____ are going to the movies.

_____ and _____ are going to the basketball game.

Look at the pictures. Can you name the couples?

_____   _____   _____

QUOTES AND SAYINGS ABOUT LOOKS	• *You can't judge a book by its cover.* • *Beauty is only skin-deep.*

Look at these pictures. Work with a classmate. Can you find 10 differences in five minutes?

Talk with a classmate. Take turns asking and answering these questions.

1. Which seems more interesting: working in an office or working outside?
2. Which would you like more: working in a busy and noisy office or working in a quiet office?

READING 14.2

Lois, the receptionist, had a busy hour. Here are the messages she took for people in her office.

Message For __MR. FORD__

Date __2/7__ Time __12:10__

Urgent		Call back at #	✓
Not urgent	✓	545-1245	
Don't call back			

Message:
MR. GOMEZ OF BIG WORLD BANK CALLED. WANTS TO SET UP MEETING.

Message For __MS. LEE__

Date __2/7__ Time __12:15__

Urgent		Call back at #	✓
Not urgent	✓	267-3722	
Don't call back			

Message:
MR. HIRATA NEEDS TO CANCEL TODAY'S MEETING. HE WANTS TO RESCHEDULE FOR TOMORROW AT 9.

Message For __MR. FORD__

Date __2/7__ Time __12:40__

Urgent	✓	Call back at #	✓
Not urgent		681-7561	
Don't call back			

Message:
YOUR DAUGHTER'S SCHOOL CALLED. SUSIE IS SICK. PLEASE PICK HER UP.

Message For __RAY__

Date __2/7__ Time __12:25__

Urgent		Call back at #	
Not urgent	✓		
Don't call back	✓		

Message:
DR. JEE'S OFFICE CALLED TO REMIND ABOUT APPOINTMENT ON FRI. AT 11.

UNDERSTANDING

A. Mr. Ford has two messages. What should he do first? Check (√) your answer.

_____ He should call 545-1245 and set up a meeting with Mr. Gomez.
_____ He should go to his daughter's school.
_____ He should call his daughter's school.
_____ He should take a coffee break.

B. True or False? Write _T_ if the sentence is true; write _F_ if the sentence is false.

_____ 1. Mr. Hirata wants to meet Ms. Lee at 9:00 on 2/7.
_____ 2. Mr. Hirata wants Ms. Lee to call back right away.
_____ 3. Ray needs to call Dr. Jee back.
_____ 4. Dr. Jee is changing Ray's appointment.

C. Read the following conversation and write a phone message.

Lois:	Sellmore Company. Good morning.
Man:	Hi, may I speak to Kim Lee?
Lois:	I'm sorry. Ms. Lee isn't in the office at the moment. Can I give her a message?
Man:	Yes. Please tell her that Mr. Bond called to reschedule our meeting today. I can't meet her at 2 but I can meet at 3.
Lois:	I'll give her the message. Do you want her to call you back?
Man:	Yes. It's very important that I talk to her as soon as possible.
Lois:	And what is your number?
Man:	466-3232 extension 123.
Lois:	466-3232 extension 123. I'll give her the message.
Man:	Thank you.
Lois:	Have a good day.

Message For _____

Date _____ Time _____

Urgent		Call back at #	
Not urgent			
Don't call back			

Message:

_____
_____
_____

BEFORE READING 14.3

A. Look at the title of the article and the pictures. What do you think this article is about? Check (√) your guess. (Hint: *QWERTY* is not an English word. Look at the pictures to see what it is.)

_____ why the typist's job is difficult
_____ why more people use computers now
_____ why the typewriter keyboard looks that way
_____ how to type on different keyboards

B. Do you type? How fast can you type?

READING 14.3

QWERTY? Why?

1 Look at a typewriter keyboard. On most typewriters (using a
5 Roman alphabet), there are four rows. The top row has numbers. The second row has the
10 letters *Q W E R T Y U I O P*. The third row has the letters *A S D F G H J K L*. The fourth row has the letters *Z X C V B N M*. (There may be small differences for different languages.) Why does the keyboard look like this? There is no alphabet in the
15 world like this!

To understand why the keyboard looks like this, you need to look at the history of the typewriter. In the early 1800s, there were many kinds of keyboards. Some looked like pianos with one long row. Some had
20 two rows. Some had three rows. One had ten rows! They usually had letters in the order of the alphabet, *A B C D E F G* and so on.

There were problems with all these keyboards. One problem was that the keys jammed if the typist typed
25 very quickly.

In 1872, Charles Sholes had an idea. He looked at English words and planned a new keyboard. With his new keyboard, the typist used the right hand and left hand equally. He believed that with equal
30 use of the right hand and left hand, the keys would not jam. He also believed his new keyboard helped typists type more quickly. Soon, all typewriters used Sholes' QWERTY keyboard.

Not everyone was happy. In 1930, a man named
35 August Dvorak studied the English language and planned a new keyboard. On his keyboard, he put the letters E, T, and S in the third row, close to the typist's fingers. He did this because these letters are in many English words. He believed his new keyboard was better than the QWERTY keyboard
40 because typists could type 35% faster and the keys did not jam. He was right.
45 However, people do not change easily. Most people believe the QWERTY

keyboard won't ever change.
50

VOCABULARY

alphabet _n._ all the letters in a language in a fixed order
equal _adj._ the same
to jam _v._ (of parts of a machine) to come together so nothing can move
problem _n._ something difficult or bad; something that doesn't work right

AFTER READING 14.3

A. Look at your guess on page 98. Were you correct?

B. The first paragraph in a reading often tells you what the article is about. Look at paragraph 1. Which sentence (or question) tells you what the article is about? Underline it.

> Look at a typewriter keyboard. On most typewriters (using a Roman alphabet), there are four rows. The top row has numbers. The second row has the letters *Q W E R T Y U I O P*. The third row has the letters *A S D F G H J K L*. The fourth row has the letters *Z X C V B N M*. (There may be small differences for different languages.) Why does the keyboard look like this? There is no alphabet in the world like this!

C. After the first paragraph, the article tells the history of the keyboard in time order. What happened first? second? third? Write 1 next to the first thing, 2 next to the second thing, and so on.

_____ People do not want to change. They want to keep the QWERTY keyboard.
_____ There were many kinds of keyboards, some with one row and some with ten rows!
_____ Dvorak made a better keyboard.
_____ Everyone started to use the QWERTY keyboard.

LOOKING AT LANGUAGE

A. *Some keyboards looked like pianos.*
How many rows did this keyboard have? _____

To *look like* means to have a similar look.
Who do you look like, your mother or your father? I look like

_____.

What does this picture look like? It looks like a _____

B. *In the <u>early</u> 1800s, there were many kinds of keyboards. Check (√) your answers below.*

The <u>early</u> 1800s is
_____ 1800-1830 _____ 1850-1860 _____ 1870-1899
The <u>late</u> 1800s is
_____ 1800-1830 _____ 1850-1860 _____ 1870-1899

C. *They usually had letters in the order of the alphabet, A B C D E F G and so on. And so on means that it continues in the same way. Here, and so on means H I J K L M N O P Q R S T U V W X Y Z. And so on and etc. mean the same thing.*

She is thinking about names for her baby that begin with A: Alicia, Ann, Alex, *and so on.*
What does *and so on* mean here? _____

She wants to buy things for her office--desks, chairs, typewriters, *etc.* What does *etc.* mean here?
_____

99

CHALLENGE

Do you have a good memory? Look at the picture of an office for five seconds. Then, cover the picture and answer the questions. Don't look back at the picture. If you get 7 out of 10 answers right, you have a good memory.

1. How many women are in the office? _____
2. What time is it in the office? _____
3. How many phones are there in the office? _____
4. Is there a fax machine in the office? _____
5. How many computers are in the office? _____
6. Is there paper in the typewriter? _____
7. Is the man wearing a tie? _____
8. How many people are talking on the phone? _____
9. What is outside the window? _____
10. What is the name of the company? _____

HORIZONS INC.

| QUOTES AND SAYINGS ABOUT WORK | • *Another day, another dollar.*
 • *Thinking is the hardest work.* |

Fables are stories that have a message. Aesop, a Greek fable writer, told this fable more than 2000 years ago.

The Lion and the Mouse

1 Near a river, in the bright sunshine, was a big lion. The lion was asleep.

Suddenly, a little mouse ran across its paw. The lion opened one eye.

5 Then its other eye. It looked at the mouse and remembered that it was hungry. The lion was ready to eat the little mouse.

Quickly, the mouse said, "Please, let me go. Let me go. I promise that if I can, one day, I'll help you."

The lion laughed.

10 "You are going to help me. How? When? Where? You are just a weak, little   mouse." He laughed and said, "You can never help me."

But, lucky for the mouse, the lion had a good heart and a sense of humor. He let the little mouse go.

The next day, the lion had a problem. There was a net near the river

15 and the lion walked into it but he couldn't get out. The net was very strong and 15 very big. The lion roared but how could someone help him? If a big and strong lion couldn't get out, who could help?

The little mouse heard the lion's roar.

"Shhhh," said the mouse. "I can help you." Using his sharp teeth, the little mouse cut the net

20 and the lion walked out.

"You laughed at me," said the mouse. "You didn't think I could ever help you!"

Number the pictures below from 1-7 to show what happened in the story.

Here is another fable.

The Man and the Snake

1   One day, a young man had a problem. He wanted to cross the river, but he didn't have a boat, and he didn't know how to swim either. He looked at the river. He couldn't walk across. The river was too deep.

5   A snake saw the man and said, "Good day, sir. You look sad. What's the problem?"

The man didn't want to answer at first. He wanted to run away because he knew some snakes are dangerous.

"Don't worry," said the snake. "I won't hurt you.
10 Maybe I can help you."

"Help me?" said the man. "How can a snake help a man?"

"Tell me what is wrong," said the snake.

The man said quickly, "I need to cross the river but I can't swim and I don't have a boat."

15 "I can help," said the snake. "Hold on to me and I will swim and take you across the river."

"Hold on to you? You're going to bite me!" said the man and he started to walk away.

"Stop! I'm not going to hurt you. Don't worry."

Finally, the man agreed. The man held on to the snake and they both went into the water. In the middle of the river, the snake turned around and bit the man.

20 The man cried, "Why did you bite me? I believed you."

The snake said, "Why did you believe me? I'm a snake. A snake has to be a snake. "

Number the pictures below from 1-5 to show what happened in the story.

TALK ABOUT IT

Are the messages of "The Lion and the Mouse" and "The Man and the Snake" similar or different?

What kind of weather is typical of your hometown (the place where you grew up)? Check (√) the pictures which show the weather of that place.

hot and humid

hot and dry

rainy

cold and windy

windy

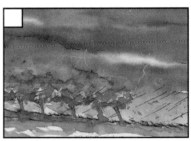

stormy

warm but not hot

cool but not cold

Circle your favorite kind of weather.

Talk with a classmate. Take turns asking and answering these questions.

1. What is the weather like in your hometown in January?
2. What is the weather like in your hometown in August?
3. What is your favorite kind of weather?
4. What month has the best weather in your hometown?

READING 16.1

Here are three postcards Roni received from her students last year.

DEAR RONI,

WHAT A GREAT PLACE! THE WEATHER IS PERFECT
WARM WITH A LIGHT BREEZE, NOT VERY HUMID.
THE BEACHES ARE PERFECT-- WHITE SAND,
COOL WATER, NOT MANY PEOPLE.

I NEVER WANT TO LEAVE HAWAII!

       BEST WISHES,
       CARLOS

RONI LEBAUER
222 MAIN ST.
LAGUNA BEACH, CA
92651

Dear Roni,

I can't believe how hot it is! Hot and dry!
Every five minutes, I drink another glass
of water.

You told me not to go to Joshua Tree Park
in July but I didn't listen. I wanted to see
a desert before I returned home.

Well...it is interesting and beautiful in
a different way. Very quiet and peaceful.

Five minutes? Time for another glass of
water!

      See you soon,
      Gia

Ms. Roni Lebauer
222 Main St.
Laguna Beach, CA
92651

Dear Roni,

It's good to be home! Southern California
was beautiful but I missed my family and
the four season weather of Vermont.

Winter here is so beautiful. The mountains
are full of snow, and the air is clean. I love to
return to my house, and sit by the fireplace
with a cup of hot chocolate.

I hope you can visit one day!

      Love,
      Emily.

Roni Lebauer
222 Main St.
Laguna Beach, CA
92651

UNDERSTANDING

A. Look at these three cartoons. Match the cartoon to the person.

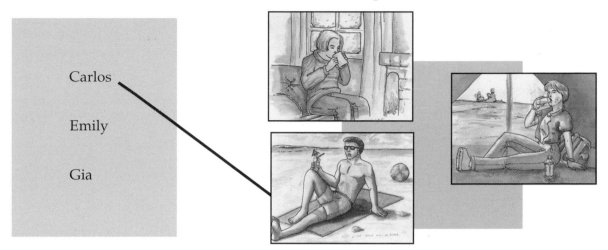

Carlos

Emily

Gia

B. True or False? Write *T* if the sentence is true. Write *F* if the sentence is false.

_F_ 1. Emily's home is in Southern California.
_____ 2. Carlos thinks Hawaii is very windy.
_____ 3. Emily likes to live in places where the seasons are very different.
_____ 4. Roni doesn't think it is a good idea to go to Joshua Tree Park in July.
_____ 5. Gia is very unhappy in Joshua Tree Park.

VOCABULARY

Look at the pictures. There is a mistake in each description. Find the mistake and cross it out.

1. The girl looks happy ~~and cold.~~

2. The woman is carrying an umbrella because it is rainy. It is hard to carry the umbrella because it is very windy and sunny.

3. The two men are enjoying the hot, cloudy day. The sun is shining.

4. Don't go outside. It looks stormy. It's not raining yet but the clouds are dark and it's very windy.

5. The children are happy because it is warm and snowy. They're playing outside and building a snowman.

READING 16.2

Where would you like to be on Sunday? On Monday?

The Weather Report

	Sunday			Monday		
	Lows	Highs	Weather	Lows	Highs	Weather
NORTH AMERICA						
Los Angeles	60° F (15° C)	77° F (25° C)	Early morning clouds; clear and sunny in afternoon	50° F (10° C)	70° F (21° C)	Cloudy with 20% chance of rain in evening.
New York	75° F (24° C)	92° F (33° C)	Sunny, humid; 50% chance of rain in late evening.	70° F (21° C)	91° F (32° C)	Sunny, humid; 60% chance of rain early morning.
Toronto	70° F (21° C)	84° F (29° C)	Light rain in morning. Afternoon clear and sunny.	70° F (21° C)	83° F (28° C)	Sunny; clear.
CENTRAL AND SOUTH AMERICA						
Mexico City	54° F (12° C)	72° F 22° C	Cloudy, cool.	60° F (15° C)	77° F (25° C)	Morning clouds; sunny afternoon; 10% chance of rain at night.
Sao Paulo	50° F (10° C)	79° F (26° C)	Partly cloudy. Strong winds.	49° F (9° C)	77° F (25° C)	Cloudy. Strong winds.
ASIA						
Bangkok	79° F (26° C)	91° F (32° C)	Light rain in morning Heavy rain in late afternoon.	79° F (26° C)	92° F (33° C)	Thunderstorms all day.
Hong Kong	75° F (24° C)	82° F (27° C)	Morning showers. Cloudy afternoon.	77° F (25° C)	84° F (29° C)	Clear all day. Sunny.

VOCABULARY

showers   *n.*   light rain
thunderstorm *n.*   rain with thunder and lightning

How many questions can you answer in two minutes? Write *T* if the sentence is true. Write *F* if the sentence is false.

_____ 1. It may rain in Los Angeles on Monday.
_____ 2. It is going to rain in Sao Paulo on Monday.
_____ 3. It is going to rain in Bangkok on Monday.
_____ 4. Sunday is going to be sunny and clear in Hong Kong.
_____ 5. It's going to rain on Sunday morning in Hong Kong.
_____ 6. Mexico City is going to have cool and cloudy weather on Sunday.
_____ 7. On Monday, Bangkok will be cold.
_____ 8. The low temperature in Sao Paulo on Sunday will be 50°F.
_____ 9. The high temperature in New York on Sunday will be 92°F.
_____ 10. It is going to be windy in Sao Paulo on Sunday and Monday.
_____ 11. It will be cloudy in Mexico City on Monday afternoon.
_____ 12. There is a small chance of rain in Los Angeles on Monday evening.
_____ 13. Toronto will have cloudy weather on Monday.
_____ 14. Toronto and Hong Kong will have similar weather on Monday.
_____ 15. Sao Paulo and Bangkok will have similar weather on Monday.

THINK ABOUT IT

Read the conversations and look at the weather forecast on page 106. Where do you think these people are? Write the name of the city in the blank.

Mia:	What are your plans for the weekend, John?
John:	I'm planning to go to the park with my family on Sunday morning.
Mia:	I don't know if that's a good idea.
John:	Why not?
Mia:	I think it's going to rain in the morning. I think the afternoon will be better.

John and Mia are probably in _____.

Sima:	When do you think the rain is going to stop?
Nabil:	Tonight? Tomorrow? I don't know.
Sima:	I'm getting tired of the rain. It rained all day yesterday and now today.
Nabil:	Oh! What was that?
Sima:	It was just some thunder. Don't worry.

Sima and Nabil are probably in _____.

Carla:	Hold on to your hat, Carlos!
Carlos:	Why... Now I know why!

Carla and Carlos are probably in _____.

BEFORE READING 16.3

Look at the pictures and title. What do you think this article is about? Check (√) your guess.

_____ why do people love their cats?
_____ what kind of weather do cats like?
_____ can cats forecast the weather?
_____ what kinds of cats do weather forecasters like?

READING 16.3

The Weather Forecaster or the Cat?

1 Some people turn on their TV to hear the weather forecast. Some people turn on the radio to learn about the weather. Some people
5 read the weather forecast in the newspaper. Some people look at ... their cats! Here are some superstitions around the world:

• In Scotland, some people say
10 that when a cat sneezes, it's going to rain.
• In Ireland, some people say that when a cat washes its face, it's going to rain.
15 • In Iceland, some people believe that when a cat stretches out its paws in front of it, bad weather is coming.
• In many parts of the world, people believe that when a cat eats 20 grass, rainy and stormy weather is coming.
• Some sailors believe that it is going to get windy when they see a cat chase its tail. 25
• In the Caribbean islands, some people believe that they can tell when a cyclone is coming. Before the cyclone, they say, their cats become nervous and restless. 30

Everyone knows weather forecasts are sometimes wrong. Perhaps cats know something people don't.

VOCABULARY

to chase	_v._	to run after something
cyclone	_n._	a very strong wind moving quickly in a circle
to forecast weather	_v._	to say what the weather will be
restless	_adj._	not relaxed; wanting to move around
superstition	_n._	an idea that is not based on science but on magic or tradition (for example, some people believe that black cats are unlucky)

AFTER READING 16.3

A. **Look at your guess on page 108. Were you correct?**

B. **Check (√) the answers.**

1. People try to learn about the weather by

    _____ reading a newspaper weather forecast.
    _____ listening to the radio weather forecast.
    _____ watching the TV weather forecast.
    _____ watching their cats.
    _____ all of the above.

2. Some people believe windy weather is coming when a cat

    _____ sneezes.
    _____ chases its tail.
    _____ washes its face.
    _____ eats grass.

C. **Finish the sentence.**

Some people in the Caribbean believe a cyclone is coming when _____.

LOOKING AT LANGUAGE

There are many sentences in the article that use the words *before* and *when*.

> *When a cat sneezes, it's going to rain.*
> *Before the cyclone, their cats become nervous.*

Write *before, after,* or *when*.

1. She takes a bath _____*before*_____ she goes to bed.
2. She irons the clothes _____ she washes them.
3. He washes the dishes _____ he puts them in the cabinet.
4. His hands get wet _____ he washes the dishes.
5. He goes to the bookstore _____ he wants to buy a book.

THINK ABOUT IT

Many people have superstitions. Here are some superstitions:

A black cat is unlucky.
The number 13 is unlucky.
If you break a mirror, you are going to have bad luck.
Make a wish when you see the first star of the night. Your wish will come true.

What superstitions do you have?

CHALLENGE

Can you find 16 "weather words" and 4 seasons in this puzzle? You may find the words vertically(↕), horizontally(↔), or diagonally(↙).

G	E	N	W	I	N	T	E	R	O	N	S
Y	T	E	R	A	U	H	U	M	I	D	P
C	L	E	A	R	S	U	M	U	C	S	R
H	O	T	M	M	A	N	O	I	L	P	I
W	O	L	C	P	O	D	O	P	O	R	N
I	B	E	D	O	E	E	R	W	U	I	K
N	S	R	S	T	O	R	M	Y	D	N	R
D	U	A	E	P	F	L	A	W	Y	G	E
W	M	I	L	E	R	F	W	T	I	E	L
R	M	N	E	E	Z	I	A	S	U	N	O
S	E	S	H	O	W	E	R	L	O	R	D
T	R	E	E	N	E	D	M	O	L	I	E

QUOTES AND SAYINGS ABOUT THE WEATHER	• *April showers bring May flowers.* • *Let a smile be your umbrella on a rainy day.*

Which animals do people have as pets inside their houses? Check (√) those pictures. Which animals would you like as a pet inside your house? Put a star (★) under those pictures.

dog

cat

bird

monkey

snake

rabbit

pig

fish

mouse

lion

turtle

Talk with a classmate. If your classmate has a pet, ask these questions.

1. What kind of pet do you have?
2. How old is it?
3. Who takes care of your pet?
4. Does it have a name?

If your classmate doesn't have a pet, ask these questions.

1. What pets do you think are good to have in the house?
2. What pets do you think are bad to have in the house?

READING 17.1

Survey: Do you have a house pet? Why or why not?

May Wong

"I have three songbirds. I love to listen to them. I wake up to the music of their song. I feel happy when I hear them."

Jerry Lane

"I have a snake. When it stretches, it's bigger than I am. My wife hates my snake. I like it. I like to watch people's faces when they first see my snake."

Marie Bernard

"I love cats. I would like to have ten cats. But I can't. I'm very allergic to them. When a cat comes close to me, I start to sneeze."

Aziz Wali

"I have dogs, but they aren't house pets. I don't understand why people have dogs in their houses. I don't think they are clean animals. They're good for one thing: watching the house."

Carmen Gonzalez

"I love dogs. I have three of them. One of my dogs is the mother. Two are her puppies. The mother is five years old. The puppies are only four months old. I really love them. They're always friendly and loving."

Terry Nolan

"I love animals. I have goldfish. I have two cats. I have one dog. I'm thinking about getting another dog but I don't have a lot of room in this house. Maybe I'll get a bird."

UNDERSTANDING

A. Check (√) the correct box or boxes.

	May Wong	Jerry Lane	Marie Bernard	Aziz Wali	Carmen Gonzalez	Terry Nolan
1. Who has more than one house pet?						
2. Who doesn't have a house pet?						
3. Who has one or more dogs inside or outside the house?						
4. Who has many kinds of house pets?						
5. Who is thinking about getting another house pet?						

B. Complete the sentences

1. May Wong likes birds because they can _____*sing*_____ .
2. Carmen Gonzalez likes dogs because they are _____ and _____ .
3. Aziz Wali doesn't let his dogs in the house because he thinks they aren't _____ .
4. Marie Bernard doesn't have cats because she is _____ to them.

VOCABULARY

Fill in the blanks with the animals below. You can use any animal more than one time.

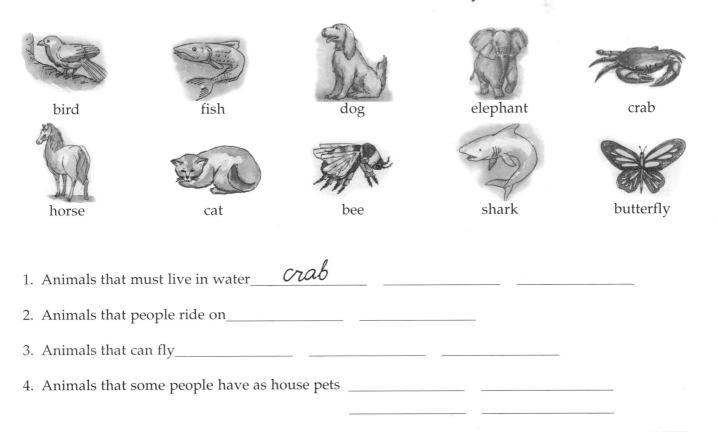

bird   fish   dog   elephant   crab

horse   cat   bee   shark   butterfly

1. Animals that must live in water ____*crab*____ _____ _____

2. Animals that people ride on _____ _____

3. Animals that can fly _____ _____ _____

4. Animals that some people have as house pets _____ _____

_____ _____

113

READING 17.2

Sometimes, people lose their pets. They try to find them by putting signs in the neighborhood. Look at these signs.

1

MISSING CAT

"Fluffy" is 3 years old. She has one green eye and one blue eye. She is brown with black stripes.
Disappeared on March 17 near the post office.
REWARD for information!
CALL 269-2424

2

DOG MISSING !!!

NAME: **SANDY**
LOST ON MARCH 9 NEAR EAST STREET. SANDY IS MEDIUM-SIZED WITH SHORT BROWN HAIR AND BLACK EYES. DON'T BE AFRAID. HE'S FRIENDLY.
REWARD: CALL JO, 303-2721.

3

LOST CAT !!

Help me find my pet cat! She is 6 years old. She has long white hair and a long tail. Her name is Snowball.
Call Mari at 630-4789

4

HELP FIND "BLACKIE"

LOST ON MARCH 3 NEAR MAIN STREET. BLACKIE IS 8 YEARS OLD, BUT HE LOOKS LIKE A PUPPY. HE'S BLACK AND WHITE WITH LONG EARS.
REWARD FOR INFORMATION. CALL SAM, 598-3985.

5

DO YOU KNOW WHERE "Lady" is ?

Lady is a black kitten -- only 6 months old. Her mother misses her!
If you know where Lady is, PLEASE CALL 303-2720

SCANNING

How many questions can you answer in two minutes? Write *T* if the sentence is true; write *F* if the sentence is false.

_____ **1.** Sandy was lost on March 6.

_____ **2.** Sandy is not friendly.

_____ **3.** There is a reward for information about Fluffy.

_____ **4.** Lady is two years old.

_____ **5.** Snowball has long hair.

_____ **6.** Lady is a mother cat.

_____ **7.** Fluffy is black with brown stripes.

_____ **8.** Sandy is a large dog.

_____ **9.** Blackie has long ears.

_____ **10.** Fluffy was lost near the hospital.

UNDERSTANDING

Read the telephone conversations. Does each caller have the right animal?

1. Jo: Hello.
   Caller: Hi. There's a dog walking around my neighborhood. Maybe it's your dog.
   Jo: What does the dog look like?
   Caller: It's medium-sized.
   Jo: Short hair or long hair?
   Caller: Short hair. White with brown spots.

   True or False?
   _____ That dog may be Sandy.

2. Man: Hello.
   Caller: Is this 303-2720?
   Man: Yes, it is.
   Caller: Did you lose a kitten?
   Man: Yes, do you have her?
   Caller: Well, I found a kitten yesterday. She's black with brown stripes.

   True or False?
   _____ That kitten may be Lady.

3. Woman: Hello.
   Caller: I'm calling about your lost cat.
   Woman: Yes? Do you have Fluffy?
   Caller: I think so. I found her on First Avenue near Main Street. She has different colored eyes and brown fur with black stripes.

   True or False?
   _____ That cat may be Fluffy.

BEFORE READING 17.3

Look at the title and the pictures. What do you think this article is about?
Check (√) your best guess.

_____ butterflies and their colors
_____ different kinds of butterflies
_____ butterflies and other animals
_____ butterflies and their travels

READING 17.3

Same Time, Same Place?

1   It's the end of August and the monarch butterflies--hundreds of millions of them-- are doing the same thing they do every year at this time. They are beginning their trip to central Mexico from Canada and the United States. Most of the butterflies get there in about six weeks.

5   Every year, these butterflies with the orange and black wings travel from different places in North America to the same mountain forests in central Mexico (about 80 miles (133 kilometers) from Mexico City). Because there are so many butterflies, the forest looks orange, not green! Every tree--every leaf, every

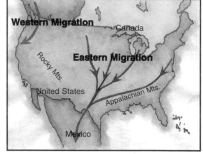

10 branch--is covered from top to bottom with butterflies. When a breeze blows, the forest seems to move!

In March, the butterflies leave their Mexican forest and travel to different places in the United States and Canada. Some go to the east coast; some go to the west coast; some go to the central areas; some go
15 to beaches; some go to forests; some go to mountains. But in August, the butterflies always go to the same place that their grandparents left seven months before.

Will the monarch butterflies make this trip next year--same time, same place? The year after? The year after that? Maybe not. Logging companies are cutting down the butterflies' forests. If their
20 logging continues, the monarch butterflies' travels--and lives--may end.

VOCABULARY

logging	*n.*	cutting down trees to sell the wood
one million	=	1,000,000

AFTER READING 17.3

A. **Look at your guess on page 116. Were you correct?**

B. **Write *T* if the sentence is true; write *F* if the sentence is false.**

    _____ 1. Monarch butterflies are orange and black.

    _____ 2. The forest in Mexico has trees with orange leaves.

    _____ 3. The monarch butterflies all go to the same place in the United States.

    _____ 4. The monarch butterflies all go to the same place in Mexico.

    _____ 5. 1,000,000 monarch butterflies go to Mexico every year.

    _____ 6. The monarch butterflies only live on the top of the trees in Mexico.

    _____ 7. The monarch butterflies know where to go in Mexico because they were there before.

C. **Check (√) your answers.**

1. Look at the title again. Why is there a question mark?

    _____ No one is sure when the butterflies travel.

    _____ No one is sure where the butterflies travel.

    _____ No one is sure if the butterflies will continue to travel in the same way.

2. Why may the monarch butterflies' trips end?

    _____ Because animals are eating them.

    _____ Because logging companies are cutting their forests.

    _____ Because they are tired of traveling.

LOOKING AT LANGUAGE

A. **Look at the first sentence.**

It's the end of August and the monarch butterflies--hundreds of millions of them--are doing the same thing they do every year at this time.

The words--*hundreds of millions of them*--are added to the main sentence. Here is the main sentence underlined.

It's the end of August and the monarch butterflies--hundreds of millions of them--are doing the same thing they do every year at this time.

Underline the main sentence below.

Every tree--every leaf, every branch--is covered from top to bottom with butterflies.

B. **Look at the circled word. What does it refer to? Draw an arrow to the word or words.**

1. The butterflies are orange and black. (They) are beautiful.

2. The monarch butterflies--hundreds of millions of (them)--are doing the same thing.

3. They are beginning their trip to central Mexico from Canada and the U. S. Most of the butterflies get (there) in about six weeks.

4. Logging companies are cutting down the butterflies' forests. If (their) logging continues, the monarch butterflies' travels may end.

CHALLENGE

How much do you know about animals? See if you can answer these questions! If you get seven or more right, you know a lot.

elephant

lion

rabbit

giraffe

black bear

whale

ostrich

turkey

penguin

ant

1. The Asian elephant lives on average
   ____ a. 100 years ____ b. 40 years ____ c. 15 years

2. The oldest pet cat was
   ____ a. 36 years old ____ b. 26 years old ____ c. 16 years old

3. The average life of a pet cat is
   ____ a. 12 years ____ b. 16 years ____ c. 20 years

4. True or False? ____ A lion can run faster than a rabbit.

5. The tallest living animal is
   ____ a. the elephant ____ b. the black bear ____ c. the giraffe

6. In 1975, an Englishman paid $17,000 for a bird. What was the bird good for?
   ____ a. eating ____ b. speaking ____ c. racing

7. The heaviest animal in the world is
   ____ a. the African elephant ____ b. the blue whale
   ____ c. the black bear

8. What living bird produces the largest egg?
   ____ a. ostrich ____ b. turkey ____ c. penguin

9. True or False? ____ Birds can see better than people.

10. The most dangerous ants in the world live in
    ____ a. Africa ____ b. Asia ____ c. Australia

QUOTES AND SAYINGS ABOUT ANIMALS	• *A dog is a man's best friend.* • *Don't count your chickens before they are hatched.*

 **W**hat do you like to do for fun? Check (√) the pictures that show those things.

"I like to watch TV."

"I like to go to the movies."

"I like to dance."

"I like to read."

"I like to go to plays."

"I like to go camping."

"I like to go to art museums."

"I like to play sports."

 Talk with a classmate. Take turns asking and answering this question.

What do you like to do for fun?

Tell the class what you and your classmate <u>both</u> like to do.

Example: *We both like to eat out.*

 **READING 18.1**

DEAR RONI,

HOW NICE TO HEAR THAT YOU WILL BE IN LONDON FOR A FEW DAYS IN JUNE. LUCKILY, I'LL BE FREE AND WE CAN SPEND SOME TIME TOGETHER.

I LOOKED IN THE NEWSPAPER AND THERE ARE A LOT OF INTERESTING THINGS TO DO. OF COURSE, THERE ARE THE MUSEUMS, OLD CHURCHES, AND TOURIST SITES. THE BRITISH MUSEUM HAS AN EXCELLENT EXHIBIT OF CHINESE PAINTING. (ONE GOOD THING ABOUT GOING TO MUSEUMS IN JUNE IS THE AIR-CONDITIONING!)

I CAN ALSO GET TICKETS FOR PLAYS IF YOU WANT. MANY PEOPLE ARE TALKING ABOUT THE PIANO LESSON, A DRAMA BY THE AMERICAN WRITER, AUGUST WILSON. THEY SAY IT'S VERY GOOD. IF YOU LIKE MUSICALS, MANY PEOPLE RECOMMEND CATS.

THE TENNIS GAMES IN WIMBLEDON BEGIN ON JUNE 22 ND. DO YOU LIKE TENNIS? TICKETS ARE VERY HARD TO GET BUT I CAN TRY.

WRITE ME SOON AND TELL ME WHAT YOU WANT TO DO. I'M LOOKING FORWARD TO SEEING YOU.

LOVE,

JON

Dear Jon,

I want to do everything! But that's not possible in four days, is it?

I love Chinese art so I would like to go to the museum. I also really like drama. If you can get tickets to _The Piano Lesson_ -- great! (I'm not a lover of musicals so I'm not interested in Cats.)

Tennis? That sounds like a lot of fun. (I love tennis. I play twice a week, but I'm not very good.) Do you think we can get tickets for a morning game?

Thank you so much for all your help. See you soon!

Love,
Roni

VOCABULARY

There are many kinds of plays. One kind is a *drama*. A drama is serious, not funny. Another kind of play is a *comedy*. A comedy is funny. Another kind of play is a *musical*. In a musical, there are songs. A musical can be a drama or a comedy.

UNDERSTANDING

A. Check (√) the pictures that show what Roni wants to do in London.

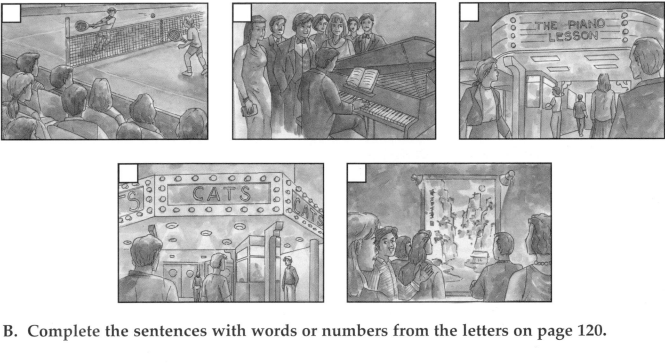

B. Complete the sentences with words or numbers from the letters on page 120.

1. Roni is going to be in London for _____ days.
2. *The Piano Lesson* is the name of a _____.
3. Wimbledon is the place where people play _____.
4. Roni doesn't like _____.
5. Jon can get _____ for *The Piano Lesson*.

VOCABULARY

There are many kinds of programs to watch on TV. Here are some:

- drama
- talk show
- game show
- news
- sports show
- cartoons
- comedy
- soap opera

Complete the sentences with the correct kind of program.

1. On this program, someone can win a lot of money. This is a _____.
2. I get very excited when I watch the tennis players and basketball players on a _____.
3. When I want to know what is happening all over the world, I watch the _____.
4. I want to laugh. I think I should turn on the TV and watch a _____.
5. _____ are for children, but sometimes adults like them too.

READING 18.2

In many newspapers, there is an entertainment page. Look at the ads on this entertainment page.

Best of the Week

Music

Jeff Gonzalez plays jazz on Sunday at 6 p.m. in Balboa Park. Free/746-3906.

The Jimmies play rock on Monday at Club 333 at 333 South St. Doors open at 6. 646-2908.

Reba Ray sings pop music on Tuesday at Carl's Place. Shows start at 7 and 9. 466-3636.

BOLTON

Michael Bolton is in town for five pop music concerts beginning on Monday. Concerts begin at 8 p.m. Monday to Friday in Balboa Stadium. 746-7878.

Juan Gabriel performs his music in Spanish and English one night only. Saturday, 9 p.m. at Balboa Stadium. 746-7878.

GABRIEL

Theater

Alone Together, Lawrence Roman's comedy about an old couple who plan to retire. Balboa Theater, Tuesday to Sunday, 8 p.m. 946-2288.

Promises, Promises, a musical comedy by Neil Simon about a man and his bosses. Grand Theater, Friday and Saturday, 2 p.m. and 8 p.m. both days. 269-6609.

Art and Photography

BURNING BUSH by Hockney

David Hockney. Twenty new paintings by artist David Hockney. Balboa Museum. Open Tuesday to Thursday, 10-5. Friday to Sunday, 10-7.

Other

The 8th International Cat Show is at the Balboa Convention Center from 9 a.m. to 5 p.m. daily. 446-9343.

SKIMMING

How many questions can you answer in two minutes?

1. I want to see Neil Simon's play. What is the name of the theater? _____.
2. When does the art museum close on Thursday? _____.
3. I want to hear rock music. Who is playing rock music? _____.
4. What time is Jeff Gonzalez playing on Sunday? _____.
5. What kind of music does Jeff Gonzalez play? _____.
6. How many concerts is Michael Bolton going to play in town? _____.
7. How many concerts is Juan Gabriel going to perform this week? _____.
8. What is the phone number for the cat show? _____.
9. I like comedies but not musicals. What play should I see? _____.
10. What kind of music does Reba Ray sing? _____.

THINK ABOUT IT

1. It's Wednesday night. Look at the entertainment page on page 122. What can you do?
   a._____
   b._____
   Which sounds better to you? _____

2. It's Saturday night. Look at the entertainment page on page 122. What can you do?
   a._____
   b._____
   c._____
   Which sounds best to you? _____

3. It's Friday at noon. Look at the entertainment page on page 122. What can you do this afternoon?
   a._____
   b._____
   c._____
   Which sounds best to you? _____

Look at the title and the pictures. What do you think this article is about?

_____

_____

_____

READING 18.3

Are We Having Fun Yet?

1 Every year, about 100 men and women do something very unusual. They say it is fun. Some people have unusual ideas about having fun!

Every year in February (since 1974), about 100 men and
5 women race up the Empire State Building in New York City. To finish the race, they have to climb 1,430 steps in a dark, narrow, and dirty stairwell. There are 102 floors in the building and racers must change stairwells at the 20th and 65th floors. The race ends at the 86th floor.

10 In 1994, Darrin Eisman, a chemist, won. He finished in 9 minutes and 37 seconds. "It was awful," he said when he finished. "The dust, the dust... the dust."

The 1994 female winner was an Australian schoolteacher, Belinda Soszyn, 39. Her time was 11 minutes and 57
15 seconds. "A bit of a sweat," she said. "And I don't usually sweat."

The last person to finish was Chico Scimone, an 83-year-old man from Italy. Scimone said he raced to see if he was living right.   He finished in 23 minutes and 20 seconds. He was happy with his time.

One runner, Maureen Nally, tried to explain why people run this race. "This is your life," she said.
20 "You have to do these things."

VOCABULARY

dust	_n._	small bits of dirt in the air
to explain	_v._	to give reasons for doing something
to sweat	_v._	to produce small drops of salty water on your skin
unusual	_adj._	not usual; something that people don't see or do very often

AFTER READING 18.3

A. Look back at your guess on page 124. Were you correct?

B. Another title for this article could be
___ A Great Building   ___ A Great Man From Italy
___ A Race Up and Up   ___ A Dirty Building

C. Match the number on the left with the words on the right.

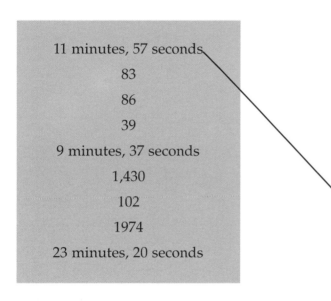

11 minutes, 57 seconds	the number of steps in the race
83	Belinda Soszyn's age
86	the last floor of the race
39	the year of the first race up the Empire State Building
9 minutes, 37 seconds	Chico Scimone's age
1,430	the number of floors in the Empire State Building
102	Chico Scimone's time to finish
1974	the winner's time to finish
23 minutes, 20 seconds	Belinda Soszyn's time to finish

LOOKING AT WORDS

A. Find four words in the reading that end with *-er* or *-ers*.

racers _____ _____ _____

The *-er* ending in these words means _____.

B. Draw a line to match each word with its opposite.

dirty	first
narrow	loser
dark	wide
female	sad
winner	clean
last	male
happy	light

THINK ABOUT IT

Does the race on page 124 sound like fun to you?

CHALLENGE

Do you know where the first modern Olympic Games were in 1896? Fill in the blanks with words from Unit 18. When you finish, read the highlighted letters going down.

1. This kind of play or movie is not funny.

2. Someone who makes art is an _____ .

3. I like to watch game _____ on TV.

4. They ran a _____ and the winner finished in two minutes.

5. I like to listen to music "live," so I enjoy _____ .

6. He is a good actor but not a good singer; he should perform in dramas, not _____

7. He lives in a _____ with 102 floors.

8. Children like to watch _____ on TV because they like to see animals talk.

9. It is hard for a two-year-old to walk up twelve _____ .

10. If you want to see a movie or a play, go to a _____ .

11. A play or movie that makes you laugh is a _____ .

12. If you want to go to a play, you usually have to buy a _____ .

QUOTES AND SAYINGS ABOUT WINNING AND LOSING	• *You can't win them all.*
	• *You win a few; you lose a few.*

Which vacation looks best to you? Check (√) the picture.

VISIT MUSEUMS!
SHOP!
EAT IN THE BEST
PLACES!
ENJOY
EXCITING
NIGHTLIFE!

SKI!!
PLAY IN THE SNOW!

SIT BY THE FIREPLACE WITH A HOT DRINK !

SWIM!
DIVE!
RELAX!

ENJOY THE SUN AND WATER!

Talk with a classmate. Take turns asking and answering these questions.

1. What sounds best to you--a vacation at the beach, a vacation in the mountains, or a vacation in a city? Why?
2. What vacation spot do you recommend in your country? Why?

127

READING 19.1

Survey: How do you like to travel?

The Satos
Retired
Japan

"We like to travel by train. The train system in Japan is excellent. You can get to small towns and big cities. There is a train called the "bullet train" that goes from Tokyo to other cities very quickly. We like the train because we can look out the window, walk around, sit back, and relax."

Michelle Ryan
Business Woman
England

"I like to travel by plane. My life is very busy and I'm always running, running, running. I love planes because I can't run. For a few hours, I just sit, read, and sleep. Someone brings me food. I never feel restless. Usually, the plane lands too soon!"

Eva Mueller
Student
Australia

"I like to travel by bicycle. Last year I took a four-month trip to the United States. I bicycled from the east coast to the west coast. My legs are pretty strong! I love bicycling and traveling because I see the country slowly. I meet people in small towns. I learn a lot... and I get great exercise!"

Albert Wong
Banker
Hong Kong

"I love cruise ships. My wife and I took a 10-day cruise last year in Greece. It is so relaxing to watch the ocean. On a cruise, you never have to worry. The food is great. You don't need to look for a hotel. You just sit back and let the captain of the ship do the work."

Ana Castillo
Doctor
Venezuela

"I hate planes. I don't like trains or buses. I get bored on cruise ships. I don't like sitting in cars for a long time. I want to move around, not sit in one place. I guess I like to travel 'by foot' !"

James Carroll
Mechanic
United States

"I enjoy traveling by car. I feel free with a car. I don't have to follow anyone's schedule. If I want to go somewhere, I go there. If I want to stop, I stop. I can play the radio loud and enjoy the music. No one tells me what to do or where to go. I like that."

YOUR TURN

How do you like to travel--by plane, by train, by car, by bus, by ship, or by foot?

UNDERSTANDING

A. Match the people with the kind of travel they prefer.

The Satos

Michelle Ryan

Eva Mueller

Albert Wong

Ana Castillo

James Carroll

B. Complete the sentences.

1. Eva likes to travel by bicycle because she can_____
   and_____.
2. Michelle likes to travel by plane because she can stop _____
3. The Satos like to travel by train because they can _____
   and_____.
4. James likes to travel by car because he feels free and doesn't have to _____.
5. _____ gets restless in cars.

VOCABULARY

Complete the sentences with words from the picture. Use each word only once.

bus

bus driver

luggage compartment

suitcase

bus station

ticket counter

ticket agent

passenger

Woman:	My wallet! I lost my wallet!
Man:	Think! Where were you? Maybe we can find it.
Woman:	Well... I got up this morning and took a taxi to the _____. I walked up to the_____ to buy a ticket. The _____ was very nice. He wanted to know all about my trip.
Man:	Did you pay him for the ticket?
Woman:	Of course! I took out my wallet and paid him. I remember that I put my wallet in my pocket.
Man:	And then?
Woman:	Then, I picked up my _____ and walked to the bus. The _____ put my suitcase in the _____. Then I got on the_____.
Man:	Was the bus crowded?
Woman:	Yes. There were many _____. There wasn't a lot of room.

What do you think happened to her wallet?

READING 19.2

Look at these three hotel brochures.

Ramana Royal Hotel

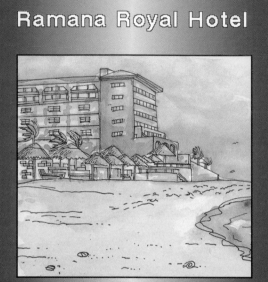

The new Ramana Royal Hotel is 10 minutes from Belize City, in a beautiful spot overlooking the Carribean Sea. It is the largest hotel in Belize and has 118 rooms, all with air-conditioning, ocean views, ceiling fans, TV's, and telephones. The hotel also has excellent restaurants, a large swimming pool, live entertainment nightly, gift shops, a beauty salon, and a sightseeing tour desk.

● ● ● ● ●

Come to the
Ramana Royal Hotel

HOLIDAY VACATION APARTMENT HOTEL

Located in Belize City on the waterfront, these 40 modern apartments will feel like home. Each apartment is furnished. One or two bedroom apartments are available. Each apartment has a kitchen, living room and bathroom. All apartments have patios with views of the water.

Visit Belize City and stay at the Holiday Vacation Apartment Hotel-- a home away from home!

FOURTH STREET GUEST HOUSE

This bed and breakfast in the center of Belize City is the perfect romantic getaway. The three-story Fourth Street Guest House was originally built in 1928 as a home for a Spanish doctor and his family. There are six guest rooms, all with different furniture. The second floor restaurant is one of the best in Belize.

Come to the
Fourth Street Guest House
You won't want to leave!

UNDERSTANDING

A. Check (√) the correct box or boxes.

	Ramana Royal Hotel	Fourth Street Guest House	Holiday Vacation Apartment Hotel
1. Which places are in Belize City?		√	√
2. Which places overlook the water?			
3. Which place is oldest?			
4. Which place is smallest?			
5. If you want to cook while you are in Belize, where should you stay?			
6. If you want to hear live music at your hotel, where should you stay?			

B. Write *T* if the sentence is true; write *F* if the sentence is false. Write *?* if the brochures don't say.

_F_   **1.** All the rooms in the Fourth Street Guest House look the same.

_____   **2.** The Fourth Street Guest House began as a hotel in 1928.

_____   **3.** Rooms at the Ramana Royal Hotel have both air-conditioning and a ceiling fan.

_____   **4.** The Ramana Royal Hotel has more than one restaurant.

_____   **5.** There are 20 one-bedroom apartments and 20 two-bedroom apartments at the Holiday Vacation Apartment Hotel.

_____   **6.** There is entertainment every night at the Ramana Royal Hotel.

THINK ABOUT IT

Which hotel sounds best to you? _____ **Why? (Check your reason or reasons.)**

_____ I like big hotels.

_____ I like to cook when I travel.

_____ I like small guest houses.

_____ I like old places.

_____ I like romantic places.

_____ I don't like living in one room; I prefer a bedroom and a living room when I travel.

_____ I like modern places.

_____ I like to be inside the city.

_____ I like to have views of the water.

_____ I like places where all the rooms are different.

_____ I like to have air-conditioning, a TV, and a telephone.

_____ I like to have a lot of services such as a gift shop, a beauty salon and a sightseeing desk at the hotel.

_____ I like to stay in hotels with a swimming pool.

Look at the title and the picture. What do you think this article is about? Check (√) your guess.

> _____ travel to the moon
> _____ travel to the South Pole
> _____ travel to the North Pole
> _____ traveling alone

READING 19.3

Travels to the End of the Earth

¹ At age nine in her native New Zealand, Helen Thayer climbed her first mountain peak. Forty five years later, Thayer and her husband, Bill, traveled to the North Pole--on skis, pulling their own sleds! Helen Thayer became the first
⁵ woman to do this. Bill Thayer, at 66 years old, became the oldest man to do this.

To prepare for their trip, Helen and Bill exercised daily. They began each day with a long run, followed by an hour of lifting weights. After lunch, they kayaked for an hour. Then
¹⁰ they pulled heavy sleds uphill for an hour.

The Thayers started their trip on March 5, 1992 at Resolute Bay, 600 miles (1000 kilometers) above the Arctic Circle. From there, they pulled 250 pound (113 kilogram) sleds as they walked and skied over the ice. They carried everything with them. No snowmobiles or air-planes followed them. They slept in a tent.   Two months--and nearly 800 miles (1333 kilometers)--later
¹⁵ they reached the North Pole.

During those two months, the temperature went down to -70 degrees Fahrenheit (-56 degrees Celsius) and never went higher than -15 degrees Fahrenheit (-26 degrees Celsius). Once, Helen Thayer's eyes froze shut.

There were difficult moments--very strong winds, snowstorms. They "met" polar bears but they were
²⁰ careful --and lucky; they didn't get hurt.

Are Helen and Bill ready to retire now? No. The South Pole might be their next trip!

VOCABULARY

to freeze (past tense=froze)	_v._	to change a liquid (like water) to something hard (like ice)
kayak	_n._	a narrow boat for one or two people
moutain peak	_n._	the highest point of a large hill
polar bear	_n._	a large white bear
ski	_n._	a long, thin metal strip attached to each foot
sled	_n._	a vehicle on runners, pulled on snow

AFTER READING 19.3

A. Look back at your guess on page 132. Were you correct?

B. There are six paragraphs in this article. Number them.

1. Which paragraph tells about how the Thayers got ready for their trip? Paragraph _____.
2. Which paragraphs tell about their trip? Paragraphs _____ and _____ and _____.
3. Which paragraph tells about their future plans? Paragraph _____.

C. Check (√) the correct pictures.

1. Which picture shows the Thayers during their trip?

2. What did the Thayers do to prepare for the trip?

3. What were their difficult moments?

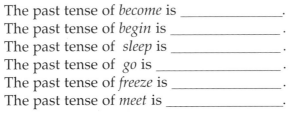

D. How old was Helen when she traveled to the North Pole? _____

LOOKING AT LANGUAGE

A. Many words in the reading are in the past tense. Most past-tense words have an -ed ending but some are irregular. Look through the article and find the irregular past-tense words.

The past tense of *become* is _____.
The past tense of *begin* is _____ .
The past tense of *sleep* is _____ .
The past tense of *go* is _____ .
The past tense of *freeze* is _____.
The past tense of *meet* is _____ .

B. Look at the circled word. What does it refer to? Draw an arrow to the word or words.

1. Helen and Bill Thayer are not retired. They are ready for their next trip.
2. Helen and Bill Thayer traveled to the North Pole--on skis, pulling their own sleds. Helen Thayer became the first woman to do this.
3. To prepare for their trip, Helen and Bill exercised daily.
4. The Thayers "met" polar bears but they were careful--and lucky; they didn't get hurt.

 **CHALLENGE**

The Browns, the Whites, and the Greens just left the travel agency. They all bought tickets to different places. One problem--they all left with the wrong tickets! Can you figure out each couple's travel plans--the place, the time, and the kind of transportation?

1. Jane Brown left the agency with tickets to Japan.
2. Lidia Green left the agency with tickets to San Francisco.
3. The flight to Paris is in April.
4. Jane Brown is glad she's not going to the United States.
5. Sima White can only travel in December.
6. The flight to Japan is in December.
7. Sima White only travels by train.

Complete the sentences with the correct information.

Example: The Lanes are going to travel to New York in June by car.

The Browns are going to travel to _____ in _____ by _____.
The Whites are going to travel to _____ in _____ by _____.
The Greens are going to travel to _____ in _____ by _____.

SAYINGS ABOUT TRAVEL AND TRANSPORTATION	• *Travel broadens the mind.* • *Travel is the best teacher.*

What do you see in these pictures? Are you sure?

The story of the blind men and the elephant is a simple story with an important moral. (A moral is the message or lesson of the story.)

The Blind Men and The Elephant

1   "An elephant is coming to town! The traveling circus is coming to town and they're going to bring an elephant," the storekeeper told all her customers. This was
5 the first elephant to come to this town and everyone was excited.

    In this town, there were three blind men. They, too, were excited. They wanted to touch the elephant. They couldn't see with
10 their eyes but they could use their hands to "see".

    Finally, the day came. Everyone woke up early to see the elephant.

    The first blind man went near the
15 elephant and touched its trunk. He moved his hand up and down the trunk "Hmmm," he thought, "now I know what an elephant looks like."

    The second blind man went near one of the animal's legs and touched it. He moved his hand up and down the leg. "Hmmm," he thought, "now I know what an elephant
20 looks like."

    The third blind man went near the animal's tail and touched it. "Hmmm," he thought, "now I know what an elephant looks like."

trunk

leg

tail

THINK ABOUT IT

What happened next?

Later that day, the three blind men met in the street. They were excited about "seeing the elephant.

25   "It was like a very big snake," said the first man. "Its skin was rough."

"Like a snake? It was like the trunk of a tree," said the second man. "But you're right about the skin. It was rough."

"Like a snake? Like the trunk of a tree? You're both wrong. It was like a snake but like a small snake... and it had hair on the end!"

30   Each man thought he was right and walked away, shaking his head at the stupidity of the other two.

Moral: Your view of life may change if you take a step to the right or left.

UNDERSTANDING

Number the pictures below from 1-6 to show what happened in the story.

TRY IT

Work in groups of five to read this story to the class. One person is the first blind man; one person is the second blind man; one person is the third blind man; one person is the storekeeper; one person is the narrator.

THINK ABOUT IT

Three people go to your country but they go to different parts of the country. What are three different views they might get of your country?

Unit 1

1. a 2. d 3. b 4. c 5. a
6. d 7. a 8. b 9. d 10. c

Unit 2

Millie Wu's favorite subject is English.
Malka Barak's favorite subject is art.
Sima Odeh's favorite subject is history.
Boris Anders' favorite subject is math.
James Monroe's favorite subject is psychology.

Unit 3

Across clues:

3. name 4. retired 7. brother 10. nap
11. grandson 12. phone 13. bride

Down clues:

1. mother 2. independence 5. problem
6. daughter 8. twins 9. dawn

Unit 4

R	V	A	T	F	B	B	A	D	O	C	T	O	R	C	F	C
S	A	W	T	O	A	A	L	N	E	G	R	O	O	P	M	A
E	T	A	C	T	O	R	K	B	E	N	G	I	N	E	E	R
F	T	I	T	E	R	B	M	E	C	R	T	L	A	N	C	P
L	E	T	I	L	N	E	R	E	R	C	M	I	T	L	H	E
O	A	E	P	L	A	R	E	S	R	O	T	T	S	J	A	N
R	C	H	R	E	C	E	P	T	I	O	N	I	S	T	N	T
I	H	A	O	R	S	A	O	N	R	K	E	U	T	C	I	E
S	E	C	R	E	T	A	R	Y	L	Y	R	E	R	O	C	R
T	R	A	R	T	N	E	T	A	I	L	O	R	S	S	L	O
P	L	I	T	D	I	V	E	R	S	B	U	T	C	H	E	R
O	P	I	L	O	T	S	R	E	C	A	S	H	I	E	R	N
S	T	A	P	A	I	N	T	E	R	J	A	N	I	T	O	R

Unit 6

1. F 2. T 3. T 4. T 5. T 6. F 7. T 8. F 9. T 10. F

Unit 7

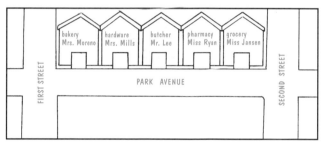

Mrs. Moreno owns the bakery.
Mrs. Mills owns the hardware store.
Mr. Lee owns the butcher store.
Miss Ryan owns the pharmacy.
Miss Jansen owns the grocery store.

Unit 8

Across clues:

1. fireplace 3. heavy 5. penthouse 6. light 7. pink 8. kitchen 10. apartment

Down clues:

1. floor 2. color 3. hospital 4. yellow 5. painter 9. home

Unit 9

	Saturday		Sunday	
9:00 a.m.	Visit Marina	9:00 a.m.	Museum of Modern Art	
10:00 a.m.		10:00 a.m.		
11:00 a.m.		11:00 a.m.	bus tour of the city	
12:00 p.m.	haircut	12:00 p.m.		
1:00 p.m.		1:00 p.m.		
2:00 p.m.	shopping for gifts	2:00 p.m.		
3:00 p.m.		3:00 p.m.		
4:00 p.m.		4:00 p.m.		
5:00 p.m.		5:00 p.m.		
6:00 p.m.		6:00 p.m.		
7:00 p.m.		7:00 p.m.		
8:00 p.m.	theater	8:00 p.m.	theater	
9:00 p.m.		9:00 p.m.		

Unit 11

A	B	B	L	U	E	D	R	O	S	S	Y	G
C	D	S	L	B	L	O	U	S	E	E	E	R
W	F	H	G	A	R	H	P	U	R	P	L	E
H	J	O	I	T	C	O	J	I	K	A	L	E
I	A	R	L	H	S	K	W	T	M	N	O	N
T	C	T	N	R	O	P	O	N	P	T	W	S
E	K	S	T	O	C	K	I	N	G	S	I	J
R	E	D	T	B	K	U	W	N	A	K	B	E
C	T	S	W	E	A	T	E	R	K	I	D	A
E	N	O	P	O	R	A	N	G	E	R	E	N
O	D	R	E	S	S	S	H	I	R	T	E	S

Unit 12

Across clues:
1. chin   3. dosage   4. sports   5. tsp
7. gym   10. stand   11. ache   12. breathe

Down clues:
2. healthy   6. soccer   8. meal   9. relax   10. such

Unit 13

Lee and Maria are going to the movies. (Drawing #1)
Joe and Celia are going dancing. (Drawing #2)
Ken and Kim are going to the basketball game. (Drawing #3)

Unit 14

1. three   2. 3:00   3. two   4. no   5. one   6. yes
7. yes   8. two   9. buildings   10. Horizons Inc.

Unit 16

G	E	N	W	I	N	T	E	R	O	N	S
Y	T	E	R	A	U	H	U	M	I	D	P
C	L	E	A	R	S	U	M	U	C	S	R
H	O	T	M	M	A	N	O	I	L	P	I
W	O	L	C	P	O	D	O	P	O	R	N
I	B	E	D	O	E	R	W	U	I	K	
N	S	R	S	T	O	R	M	Y	D	N	R
D	U	A	E	P	F	L	A	W	Y	G	E
W	M	I	L	E	R	F	W	T	I	E	L
R	M	N	E	E	Z	I	A	S	U	N	O
S	E	S	H	O	W	E	R	L	O	R	D
T	R	E	E	N	E	D	M	O	L	I	E

Unit 17

1. b   2. b   3. a   4. T   5. c
6. c   7. c   8. a   9. T   10. c

Unit 18

1. drama   2. artist   3. shows   4. race   5. concerts
6. musicals   7. building   8. cartoons   9. steps
10. theater   11. comedy   12. ticket

Reading down, the highlighted words say "Athens, Greece."

Unit 19

The Browns are going to travel to Paris in April by plane.
The Whites are going to travel to San Francisco in December by train.
The Greens are going to travel to Japan in December by plane.